THE
MICHELIN
GUIDE

CHICAGO

D1613580

MICHELIN

THE MICHELIN GUIDE'S COMMITMENTS

Whether they are in Japan, the USA, China or Europe, our inspectors apply the same criteria to judge the quality of each and every establishment that they visit. The MICHELIN guide commands a **worldwide reputation** thanks to the commitments we make to our readers—and we reiterate these below:

Our inspectors make **anonymous visits** to restaurants to gauge the quality of cuisine offered to the everyday customer. They pay their own bill and make no indication of their presence. These visits are supplemented by comprehensive monitoring of information—our readers' comments are one valuable source, and are always taken into consideration.

Our choice of establishments is a completely **independent** one, made for the benefit of our readers alone. Decisions are discussed by inspectors and editor, with the most important considered at the global level. Inclusion in the Guide is always free of charge.

The Guide offers a **selection** of the best restaurants in each category of comfort and price. A recommendation in the Guide is an honor in itself, and defines the establishment among the "best of the best."

All practical information, the classifications, and awards are revised and updated every year to ensure the most **reliable information** possible.

The standards and criteria for the classifications are the same in all countries covered by the MICHELIN guides. Our system is used worldwide and easy to apply when selecting a restaurant.

As part of Michelin's ongoing commitment to improving **travel and mobility**, we do everything possible to make vacations and eating out a pleasure.

THE MICHELIN GUIDE'S SYMBOLS

Our inspectors are experts at finding the best restaurants and invite you to explore the diversity of the gastronomic universe. As well as evaluating a restaurant's cooking, we also consider its décor, the service and the ambience – in other words, the all-round culinary experience.

Two keywords help you make your choice more quickly: red for the type of cuisine, gold for the atmosphere.

Italian • Elegant

FACILITIES & SERVICES

🍇	Notable wine list
🍸	Notable cocktail list
🍺	Notable beer list
🍶	Notable sake list
BYO	Bring your own
♿	Wheelchair accessible
⛱	Outdoor dining
⊡	Private dining room
🍳	Breakfast
🍽	Brunch
🥢	Dim sum
🅿	Valet parking
💵	Cash only

AVERAGE PRICES

$	Under $25
$$	$25 to $50
$$$	$50 to $75
$$$$	Over $75

STARS

Our famous one ✿, two ✿✿ and three ✿✿✿ stars
identify establishments serving the highest quality
cuisine – taking into account the quality of ingredients,
the mastery of techniques and flavors, the levels of
creativity and, of course, consistency.

✿✿✿   Exceptional cuisine, worth a special journey
✿✿   Excellent cuisine, worth a detour
✿   High quality cooking, worth a stop

BIB GOURMAND

Inspectors' favorites for good value.

MICHELIN PLATE

Good cooking.
Fresh ingredients, capably
prepared: simply a good meal.

DEAR READER,

It's been an exciting year for the entire team at the MICHELIN guides in North America, and it is with great pride that we present you with our 2019 edition to Chicago. Over the past year our inspectors have extended their reach to include a variety of establishments and multiplied their anonymous visits to restaurants in our selection in order to accurately reflect the rich culinary diversity this great city has to offer.

As part of the Guide's highly confidential and meticulous evaluation process, our inspectors have methodically eaten their way through the entire city with a mission to marshal the finest in each category for your enjoyment. While they are expertly trained professionals in the food industry, the Guides remain consumer-driven and provide comprehensive choices to accommodate your every comfort, taste, and budget. By dining and drinking as "everyday" customers, they are able to experience and evaluate the same level of service and cuisine as any other guest. This past year has seen some unique advancements in Chicago's dining scene. Some of these can be found in each neighborhood introduction, complete with photography depicting our favored choices.

Our company's founders, Édouard and André Michelin, published the first MICHELIN guide in 1900, to provide motorists with useful information about where they could service and repair their cars as well as find a good quality meal. In 1926, the star-rating system was introduced, whereby outstanding establishments are awarded for excellence in cuisine. Over the decades we have made many new enhancements to the Guide, and the local team here in Chicago eagerly carries on these traditions.

As we take consumer feedback seriously, please feel free to contact us at: michelin.guides@michelin.com. You may also follow our Inspectors on Twitter (@MichelinGuideCH) and Instagram (@michelininspectors) as they eat their way around town. We thank you for your patronage and truly hope that the MICHELIN guide will remain your preferred reference to Chicago's restaurants.

CONTENTS

CHICAGO

ANDERSONVILLE, EDGEWATER & UPTOWN

LINCOLN SQUARE · RAVENSWOOD

A walk through Chicago's North side, rich with culinary traditions from centuries of immigrant settlers, is like globe-trotting. A number of local businesses, specialty stores, row houses, and hotels populate the quaint streets of Andersonville, and architecture buffs never grow weary of the numerous art deco buildings set along Bryn Mawr Avenue and Lake Michigan's beaches.

HOW SWEDE IT IS

A water tower emblazoned with the blue-and-yellow Swedish flag rises above Clark Street, proudly representing Andersonville's Nordic roots. Step inside the Swedish-American Museum for a history lesson. Then browse the items on offer at one of the last Swedish emporiums in the area—**Wikstrom's Specialty Foods**. In existence for 50 years, it is now a purely online venture, boasting such classic treats as red fish, herring, and meatballs among other packaged goods. Most early birds can be found lining up for coffee and creative breakfast plates (sassy eggs or frazzled eggs, anyone?) at **Over Easy Café**, while heartier appetites won't be able to resist the Viking breakfast at **Svea Restaurant** featuring piles of Swedish-style pancakes, sausages, and toasted limpa bread.

Beyond the well-represented Scandinavian community, Andersonville also brings the world to its doorstep thanks to those amply stocked shelves at **Middle East Bakery & Grocery**. Their deli selection includes a spectrum of spreads, breads, olives, and hummus, thereby making it entirely feasible to throw a meze feast in a matter of minutes. However, if your tastes run further south (of the border), then **Isabella Bakery** is a gem for all things Guatemalan—and turns out a host of tamales to die for. Adventurous foodies depend on the grocery section to keep their pantries stocked with fresh spices, dried fruits, rosewater, nuts, teas, and more.

AN ASIAN AFFAIR

Across town, the pagoda-style roof of the Argyle El stop on the Red Line serves as another visual clue to the plethora of eats available here. Imagine an East Asian lineup of Chinese, Thai, and Vietnamese restaurants, noodle shops, delis, bakeries, and herbalists. Platters of lacquered, bronzed duck and pork make **Sun Wah BBQ** an inviting and popular spot for Cantonese cuisine, while **dak Korean** is a perpetual cult favorite for spicy chicken wings and rice bowls served from a counter. And for those less inclined to cook for themselves, a genesis of casual eateries is prospering along these streets. **BopNgrill,** for

instance, specializes in Asian fusion food like loco moco, as well as signatures like the fantastically messy kimchi burger, featuring caramelized kimchi, a fried egg, sharp cheddar, bacon, and spicy mayo. Finally, make sure to stop by **Little Vietnam** on Bryn Mawr for affordable salads, sandwiches, and that divine bowl of steaming pho.

MEAT, POTATOES —AND MORE

Chicagoans can't resist a good sausage, so find them giving thanks regularly to the German immigrants who helped develop Lincoln Square and whose appreciation for fine meats still resonates in this neighborhood. Old

World-inspired butchers ply their trade, stuffing wursts and offering specialty meats and deli items at **Gene's Sausage Shop**. For a more refined selection of chops, steaks and free-range poultry, head to **Lincoln Quality Meat Market**. Speaking of meat treats, **Wolfy's** serves one of the best red-hots in Uptown, piling its dogs with piccalilli, pickles, peppers, and other rainbow-colored condiments. Its iconic neon sign (a crimson frankfurter jauntily pierced by a pitchfork) only intensifies the urge to stop here.

For dinner party essentials, (think vegetables, fruits, flowers and more), Andersonville boasts a farmer's market in most areas and most days of the week. However, the **Andersonville Farmer's Market** in particular (held on Wednesdays) is home to an impressive number of bakeries, as well as an orchard's worth of Asian fruit. Then of course there's the **Lincoln Square Farmer's Market**, which throws its doors open like clockwork on Tuesdays, and hosts live music during market hours every Thursday evening. And also settled in Lincoln Square is **HarvesTime Foods**, a culinary bazaar that wears its sustainability on its sleeve. Imagine a solar-paneled roof set above a massive lineup of regionally sourced produce and you know that you've arrived at the right spot.

Along the same lines, Edgewater's **Sauce and Bread Kitchen** (which is a collaboration between beloved artisans **Co-op Sauce** and **Crumb Chicago**) brings two of the Windy City's favorite local products together at one location (read: café). Made-to-order breakfast and lunch sandwiches filled with maple sausage or applewood-smoked turkey are lavished with house-made condiments like tomato sauce (a fan favorite and fittingly so), while other party treats like hot sauce have a near-cultish following.

RAISE A GLASS

Critically acclaimed as one of the country's best boutique coffee shops, **The Coffee Studio** pours a mean cup of joe. Their locally roasted brews pair perfectly with a box of the "glazed & infused" doughnuts, which may need to be ordered in advance. In Edgewater, the creative community convenes at **The Metropolis Café**, an offshoot of Chicago's own **Metropolis Coffee Company**. Searching for something stronger than caffeine to bring to your next reservation? As the name suggests, family-owned producers and small-batch offerings are the focus at **Independent Spirits Inc.**, a wine and liquor shop replete with global selections.

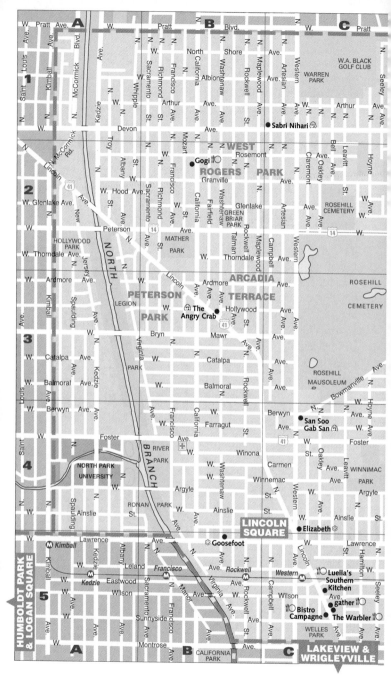

A
B
C

W. Pratt Ave.
W. Pratt Blvd.
W. Pratt

1

W. Devon Ave.

W.A. BLACK
GOLF CLUB

WARREN
PARK

North Shore Ave.
W. Arthur Ave.

● Sabri Nihari 🕌

WEST
ROGERS PARK

● Gogi 🍴

Rosemont

ROSEHILL
CEMETERY

2

W. Glenlake Ave.
W. Hood Ave.

Granville
Ave.

GREEN
BRIAR
PARK

Glenlake
Ave.

W. Peterson Ave.

HOLLYWOOD
PARK

W. Thorndale Ave.

MATHER
PARK

NORTH

ROSEHILL
CEMETERY

W. Ardmore Ave.

ARCADIA
TERRACE

W. Ardmore Ave.

3

PETERSON
PARK

🕌 The
Angry Crab ●

Hollywood
Ave.

LEGION

W. Bryn Mawr

ROSEHILL
MAUSOLEUM

W. Catalpa Ave.

W. Catalpa

W. Balmoral Ave.

W. Balmoral
Ave.

W. Berwyn. Ave.

Berwyn
Ave.

● San Soo
Gab San 🕌

4

W. Foster Ave.

NORTH PARK
UNIVERSITY

RIVER
PARK

Winona

Carmen

Winnemac
Ave.

WINNIMAC
PARK

W. Argyle

RONAN
PARK

W. Ainslie
Ave.

Argyle

Ainslie
St.

LINCOLN
SQUARE

● Elizabeth ✳

Ⓜ Kimball

W. Lawrence
Ave.

✳ Goosefoot ●

Lawrence

5

Ⓜ Kedzie

Leland

W. Eastwood
Wilson

Francisco
Ave.

🍴 Luella's
Southern
Kitchen

Ⓜ Western

🍴 gather 🍴

W. Sunnyside

🍴 Bistro
Campagne ●

● The Warbler

WELLES
PARK

A

B
CALIFORNIA
PARK

C

LAKEVIEW &
WRIGLEYVILLE

Andersonville, Edgewater & Uptown

Blvd. Pratt Blvd.
W. Columbia Ave.
N. North Shore Ave.
Clark Sheridan
Ridge Ashland Albion Glenwood Loyola Ave. LOYOLA UNIVERSITY CHICAGO
Damen Ravenswood 🍴○ Taste of Peru W. Arthur Loyola Ave.
Ave. SCHREIBER PARK Devon Ave. W. Sheridan Rd. LOYOLA UNIVERSITY CHICAGO
W. Highland Ave. Lakewood Rosemont LAKE
EMMERSON PARK Paulina Greenview Granville Granville Ave. MICHIGAN
N. Damen Ave. Hood Ave. W. Hood Ave. Broadway
Norwood St. Glenwood Glenlake Ave. W. Glenlake Ave.
Peterson Ave. Hermitage Elmdale Thorndale Sheridan EDGEWATER
St. W. Thorndale Ave. Winthrop Kenmore LANE PARK
SENN PARK 🍴○ Ras Dashen KATHY OSTERMAN BEACH
Clark Ridge 🍴 Mango Pickle W. Ardmore Ave. Rd.
Hollywood Ave. W. Hollywood Ave.
W. Ave. Olive St. N.
Bryn Mawr Lakewood Bryn Mawr Ave.
ANDERSONVILLE W. Catalpa 🍴 Jin Thai Ave.
🍴 Passerotto LAKEWOOD-BALMORAL 🍴 Herb FOSTER AVE. BEACH
🍴○ Big Jones Vincent 🍴○ Pearl's Southern Comfort 🍴○ Lake
Summerdale Balmoral Ave.
Damen Farragut W. Glenwood Berwyn Berwyn Ave. LINCOLN PARK
Ave. Wolcott 🍴○ Jin Ju Foster
Winchester 🍴 Hopleaf W. Winona Ave. Winthrop Kenmore St. MARGATE PARK
Ravenswood Winnemac Ave. Argyle 🍴○ Pho 777 UPTOWN
Ave. 🍴○ Pho Xe Tang - Tank Noodle Argyle St.
St. Ainslie St. AUGUSTINE COLL. Ainslie Sheridan Marine
N. ST. BONIFACE CEMETERY W. Clark
RAVENSWOOD 🍴○ Demera Lawrence Lawrence Ave. LINCOLN PARK
❋ Band of Bohemia CHASE PARK SHERIDAN Leland Ave.
Leland Hermitage Paulina Beacon Magnolia Wilson Wilson Ave. Halsted
Damen Wolcott PARK TRUMAN COLLEGE Broadway Rd.
Sunnyside Greenview Montrose Sunnyside Ave. CLARENDON PARK
Montrose GRACELAND CEMETERY

THE ANGRY CRAB 😳

Seafood • *Simple*

  🦽 BYO

MAP: B3

Don't be shellfish—bring friends, beer and wine to dinner at The Angry Crab for a messy, more-the-merrier experience. Lines form nightly for the chance to fill up on a Cajun-style spread shot through with Vietnamese flavors that reflect the owners' heritage.

Order from the laminated menus or the large overhead chalkboard for a seafood feast with options like whole head-on shrimp or enormous snow crab legs. Then pick from a choice of lemon, garlic or spicy sauces, stake your claim on a roll of paper towels, a seat at the communal tables and rip open the plastic bags in which the seafood arrives before digging in with your claws. Still hungry? Make it a true crab boil and add sausage, corn on the cob and red bliss potatoes to round out the feast.

🖼️ 5665 N. Lincoln Ave. (bet. Fairfield & Washtenaw Aves.)
☎ (773) 784-6848 — **WEB:** www.theangrycrabchicago.com
🖼️ Lunch Sat – Sun Dinner nightly   **PRICE:** $$

BIG JONES 🍴

Southern • *Bistro*

🍸   🏠

MAP: E3

Boasting a refreshed interior, new seats and an open kitchen equipped with extra gadgets, Big Jones greets guests with a "Guide to Good Drinking" that includes barrel-aged punch selections, as well as an impressive lineup of Bourbon and whiskey. Between that and the high-top tables, this is a guaranteed good time. Yes, it's no front porch in Louisiana, but it's certainly close.

The menu is still filled with dishes that reach back in Southern history and the staff loves to dive into ancient detail. But this does not mean that the food doesn't explain itself. Favorites that one can look forward to include homemade pimento cheese with Tasso ham cured in-house, or crawfish étouffee swimming with butter and wine and laid atop spicy, smoky Braggadocio rice.

🖼️ 5347 N. Clark St. (bet. Balmoral & Summerdale Aves.)
🚇 Berwyn
☎ (773) 275-5725 — **WEB:** www.bigjoneschicago.com
🖼️ Lunch & dinner daily   **PRICE:** $$

BAND OF BOHEMIA
Gastropub • *Rustic*

So much more than a working brewery with a talented kitchen, Band of Bohemia is in fact a truly inspired gastropub that produces its own utterly unique creations both in the glass and on the plate.

Located in a repurposed brick building across from the Metra tracks, the look is understandably industrial, with an expansive layout that unwinds into a series of seating options, inviting bar and an open kitchen with another small bar set against pretty blue tiles. Curved, high-backed booths lend intimacy to counter the room's sheer size. Stainless steel tanks displayed in the back hold the culinary-minded handiwork of their head brewer. On tap, expect a handful of rotating beers, including the thoughtful Pear Fenugreek Wheat featuring notes of pear, maple and a crisp finish.

The kitchen's boundless small and large plates defy expectations with delicious success. A fluffy omelette with osetra caviar and a savory brown butter crumble is classically French, while sweetbreads, rolled in Old Bay-seasoned breadcrumbs and served with Alabama white barbecue sauce, smack of the South. Berkshire pork chop served over a pile of kimchi, creamy labneh and compressed apple makes glorious sense.

4710 N. Ravenswood Ave. (bet. Lawrence & Leland Aves.)
Damen (Brown)
(773) 271-4710 — WEB: www.bandofbohemia.com
Lunch Sat – Sun Dinner Tue – Sun   PRICE: $$$

BISTRO CAMPAGNE

French · Bistro

MAP: C5

The romantic ideal of a French bistro is alive and well at quaint Bistro Campagne, where a tiny bar by the entrance is ready with your aperitif. Light slants through wooden Venetian blinds, bouncing off cream-and-brick walls in the welcoming dining room. Choose a white cloth-covered table inside or dine outside under the garden's twinkling lights and green tree branches.

Inspired accompaniments make for memorable versions of rustic French standards. Start with a large, savory bowl of soupe à l'oignon gratinée capped with a thick layer of melting Gruyère. Then, discover their pitch-perfect duck pithiviers, wild mushroom duxelles and hazelnuts in puff pastry with a Madeira reduction. Brown butter pain perdu tucked with black figs is moist and delicious.

▪ 4518 N. Lincoln Ave. (bet. Sunnyside & Wilson Aves.)
▪ Western (Brown)
✆ (773) 271-6100 — **WEB:** www.bistrocampagne.com
▪ Lunch Sun Dinner nightly   **PRICE:** $$

DEMERA ▮◯

Ethiopian · Simple

MAP: E5

Demera's well-lit corner location welcomes hungry Uptown residents looking to immerse themselves in Ethiopian cuisine. Colorful wicker seating at the dining room's communal table gives groups an authentic experience, while picture windows offer plenty of people-watching for everyone.

Vegetarian and omnivorous offerings abound on the menu, which also features a small glossary of terms to help newcomers. Pleasantly spicy yesiga wot combines tender chunks of beef with onions and ginger in a rich berbere sauce. Served with turmeric-infused split peas and spicy jalapeño-laced collard greens, this stew is a hearty pleasure. Sop up the extra sauce with piles of tangy and soft injera, presented in the traditional manner in lieu of silverware.

▪ 4801 N. Broadway (at Lawrence Ave.)
▪ Lawrence
✆ (773) 334-8787 — **WEB:** www.demeraethiopian.com
▪ Lunch & dinner daily   **PRICE:** $$

ELIZABETH ✿
Contemporary • Cozy

Chef Iliana Regan's unique approach to cooking at her popular Elizabeth is self-described as "New Gatherer" cuisine. Hunting and foraging are star features of this local, seasonal menu, and though her multi-course menu changes nightly (sometimes leading to subtle variations in quality) she consistently utilizes ingredients in ways that push the envelope. As proof of her talent, her popular cooking classes regularly sell out, even at $1,000 a pop.

Tucked into a bright interior, festooned with dried branches, river rocks, antlers and pottery, the décor alters with the menu. But the highlight of the space remains its fully open kitchen. Likewise, service is cheerful, warm and attentive, if a touch casual at times.

Dinner is likely to be an earthy ten—albeit manageable—course affair, and might begin with a creamy scoop of wildly fresh cheese set over sorrel purée and topped with a cloud of elderflower foam, spruce shoots and foraged plant bulbs. Later, a bread service featuring soft goat butter, crisp pork cracklings and luscious whipped lardo is memorable to say the least. At the end, a knob of turbot reaches striking new heights dressed with beurre monté and crunchy white asparagus.

▓ 4835 N. Western, Unit D (bet. Ainslie St. & Lawrence Ave.)

▓ Western (Brown)

✆ (773) 681-0651 — **WEB:** www.elizabeth-restaurant.com

▓ Dinner Tue – Sat   **PRICE: $$$$**

GATHER

American • *Neighborhood*

MAP: C5

A chic, cozy space lets guests get up close and personal at gather. Diners seeking dinner and a show take front row seats at barstools lining the open kitchen's polished granite counter, while tall communal tables fill with patrons enjoying bites from the menu's "gather and share" section. A rear dining room offers more solitude and romance.

Family-style Sunday dinners are a local draw, but the à la carte menu showcases flavorful options nightly. Slice into a single large uovo raviolo to mingle poached egg and ricotta with white truffle butter, jalapeño slivers and chopped chives, or share a crock of Pernod-splashed mussels. Fragrant and garlicky, they're served with sourdough toast points for soaking up every last drop of the white wine-cream sauce.

- 4539 N. Lincoln Ave. (bet. Sunnyside & Wilson Aves.)
- Western (Brown)
- (773) 506-9300 — **WEB:** www.gatherchicago.com
- Lunch Sat – Sun Dinner nightly   **PRICE:** $$

GOGI

Korean • *Neighborhood*

MAP: B2

The surging popularity of Korean food continues to flourish along these shores of Lake Michigan. And as foodies would have you know, Gogi is one of the best places in the city to experience it. With its hip, industrial décor, imposing exhaust fans over each table (a clear sign that there's a ton of grilling going on) and lively blend of sweet, spicy and sour flavors, dinner here promises to be a sensory explosion like no other.

One could feast on the abundant pre-meal banchan alone—a stunning selection of kimchi, mirin-soaked fish cakes, sake-steamed black beans and more. But, that would mean missing out on delicate slices of sirloin bulgogi smothered in a sweet, gingery marinade; or restorative and spicy sundubu jjigae bubbling away in an iron pot.

- 6240 N.California Ave. (bet. Granville & Rosemont Aves.)
- (773) 274-6669 — **WEB:** www.gogichicago.com
- Dinner nightly   **PRICE:** $$

GOOSEFOOT ✿

Contemporary • Chic

 ♿ BYO

This understated plate-glass façade may seem lost in a sea of mediocrity, but the restaurant it houses is truly distinct. The soothing décor appears minimal, with splashes of orange from the seating, bare tables and Rodin replicas to fashion a space that is instantly likeable. A small painting purchased by the Chef and his wife on their honeymoon in Italy graces one corner of the room. Dishes are intricate and take time to be described, which may explain the relatively slow pace of dining here.

The menu showcases classical edge and contemporary artistry. Start with a melt-in-your-mouth lobster tail puddled in citrus beurre blanc that is studded with tapioca pearls. Delicate, handmade tortellini are packed with maitake mushrooms and lovingly enhanced with fresh mint and shaved Perigord truffles. This may be followed by a slice of consommé-poached beef filet, pan-seared to medium-rare perfection and paired with enoki mushrooms, nasturtium purée and drizzled with California olive oil.

Just when you think it couldn't possibly get any sweeter, the Goosefoot experience ends with hand-crafted chocolates, a packet of seeds for your garden and a warm send-off from Chef Chris Nugent and his wife, Nina.

▨ 2656 W. Lawrence Ave. (bet. Talman & Washtenaw Aves.)
🚇 Rockwell
✆ (773) 942-7547 — **WEB:** www.goosefoot.net
▨ Dinner Wed – Sat   **PRICE: $$$$**

HERB 👻

Thai • Contemporary décor

BYO

In the sea of Thai restaurants that flank this area, elegant Herb stands out for its lovely wood and stone décor and service staff friendly enough to use your name. This is killer Thai, elevated and prepared with care.

The kitchen turns out both a three- and five-course prix-fixe dinner at tremendous value, but Chef/owner Patty Neumson's cooking is light (and delicious) enough to go the distance. A sample menu might begin with a cool pile of crunchy green papaya, carrot and cucumber, laced in a beautifully balanced lime dressing with vermicelli noodles and peanuts. Then move on to tofu and kabocha in a deliciously complex coconut curry full of wilted basil and heat. Soft glass noodles find their match in sautéed onions, fresh crab and crunchy shrimp.

- 5424 N. Broadway (bet. Balmoral & Catalpa Aves.)
- Bryn Mawr
- (773) 944-9050 — **WEB:** www.herbrestaurant.com
- Dinner Thu – Sun

PRICE: $$

HOPLEAF 👻

Gastropub • Tavern

There are so many things to love about Chicago's taverns: their complete lack of attitude; their undying hospitality; and their downright delicious cooking.

Hopleaf is a classic example of all that and more, still packing the house more than 25 years after opening. A traditional bar graces the front, but the glassed-in kitchen is where the magic happens. Named after a pale ale brewed in Malta, Hopleaf fittingly flaunts a beer list so long that it's been called "a novel."

It's hard to go wrong at this beloved gastropub, but don't miss the mussels if they're available. Another gem: the wood-grilled Duroc pork chop—a thick, juicy chop in a red wine glaze, set over white grits with smoky Gouda and accompanied by roasted cauliflower and broccoli salsify.

- 5148 N. Clark St. (bet. Foster Ave. & Winona St.)
- Berwyn
- (773) 334-9851 — **WEB:** www.hopleaf.com
- Lunch & dinner daily

PRICE: $$

JIN JU

Korean • Simple

MAP: E4

A sexy spot on a bustling stretch of North Clark, Jin Ju spins out luscious Korean classics with aplomb. Inside, dim lighting, dark wood furnishings and luxuriant fuchsia-red walls create a sophisticated coziness, while servers are gracious and attentive.

A simply named house salad showcases the restaurant's modern, accessible Korean ethos, combining meaty pan-seared portobello strips atop delicately bitter green leaf lettuce, torn sesame leaves, cucumbers and scallions in a funky garlic-soy sauce. Without tableside barbecue grills, fatty pork slabs are sautéed in the kitchen for sweetly caramelized samgyupsal. Wrapped in sesame leaves with Brussels sprouts, beets, crispy leeks and a smear of kicky miso paste, the package provides instant gratification.

 5203 N. Clark St. (at Foster Ave.)

🚇 Berwyn

✆ (773) 334-6377 — **WEB:** www.jinjurestaurant.com

 Dinner Tue – Sun   **PRICE:** $$

JIN THAI 😊

Thai • Simple

🏠 **BYO**

MAP: E3

In-the-know locals fill up on tasty Thai at this sleek corner hot spot, whose curving glass windows beckon many a passerby with views of and aromas from vibrant curries and spicy laab. Inside, a row of splashy pillows lends color and comfort to a wooden banquette, and woven placemats dress up dark wood tables.

Start a meal with zingy miang kham, featuring a betel leaf stuffed with a chopped mix of dried shrimp, fresh ginger, lime, peanuts and coconut. From there, move on to hot curry catfish or Sukothai noodle soup teeming with minced pork and steaming broth (add pinches of warm spices from the accompanying condiment tray for an even more satisfying slurp). For dessert, pick from either roti ice cream, wonton bananas or warm Thai custard.

 5458 N. Broadway (at Catalpa Ave.)

🚇 Bryn Mawr

✆ (773) 681-0555 — **WEB:** www.jinthaicuisine.com

 Lunch & dinner Wed – Mon   **PRICE:** ⬡

LUELLA'S SOUTHERN KITCHEN ⚡️○

Southern • Family

♿ 🍴 BYO

MAP: C5

Don't be fooled by the no-frills interior of this homey little soul food spot. Yes, you order at the counter; and yes, you'll be helping yourself to utensils, napkins and ice water. However, Luella's is cooking up anything but fast food. This earnest kitchen makes your order from scratch, and it's more than worth the wait. The surrounding artwork is half the fun anyway: you might even recognize prints like "Sugar Shack" by artist Ernie Barnes from the 1970's sitcom, "Good Times."

The tender buttermilk-fried chicken is a thing of beauty, served with warm collards braised with ham hock. Then pillowy biscuits, cooked to order and served with apricot jam, are pure bliss; as are Mississippi hot tamales stuffed with Slagel Farms beef and melted cheddar cheese.

▪ 4609 N. Lincoln Ave. (bet. Eastwood & Wilson Aves.)
🚇 Western (Brown)
📞 (773) 961-8196 — **WEB:** www.luellassouthernkitchen.com
▪ Lunch Tue – Sun Dinner nightly   PRICE: $$

MANGO PICKLE 😊

Indian • Colorful

MAP: E3

After nearly a decade spent traveling across India with her husband, Nakul Patel, Chef Marisa Paolillo was sufficiently inspired to return stateside and open a restaurant that celebrates its culinary diversity. Named for the country's most popular condiment, everything in Mango Pickle—from the colorful artwork and accessories to the richly layered curries—honors a deep appreciation for the South Asian country.

While dishes here riff on the classics, there are flavorful surprises at every turn. The creamy tomato-onion sauce of butter chicken is ramped up with earthy mushrooms and sundried tomatoes for a Mediterranean twist. Chana masala is spiked with ginger and garlic confit, and beef shank nihari is slow-braised in a succulent black cardamom sauce.

▪ 5842 N. Broadway (bet. Rosedale Ave. & Victoria St.)
🚇 Thorndale
📞 (773) 944-5555 — **WEB:** www.mangopicklechicago.com
▪ Dinner Wed – Sun   PRICE: $$

PASSEROTTO 🐡

Korean • *Contemporary décor*

 ♿

Cavatelli, cantuccini and crudos line the menu, but wait, isn't this a Korean restaurant? Indeed, the window advertises "fun Korean fare." However, Chef/owner Jennifer Kim honed her skills in Italian kitchens, so expect a cultural collision. It's a delightful surprise, one that welcomes a steady stream of area dwellers who arrive hungry for bright, bold and creative flavors—as seen in the Cacciucco-inspired tofu stew. Bay scallop crudo with a house-made XO sauce is another prime example of this Italian-Korean mashup. Then, pan-fried rice cakes with a lamb ragù hint at gnocchi, while Pelicana chicken is delicately fried and coated with a sweet and sticky red pepper glaze.

Despite Kim's sky-high creativity, the prices remain pleasantly down-to-earth.

▪ 5420 N. Clark St. (bet. Balmoral & Catalpa Aves.)
✆ (708) 607-2102 — **WEB:** www.passerottochicago.com
▪ Dinner Tue – Sat   **PRICE: $$**

PEARL'S SOUTHERN COMFORT 🍴

Southern • *Tavern*

🍺 ♿ 🚻 🥡

Chicago's been on a Southern food kick of late, and this sparkling Andersonville charmer is a straight up hepcat. Its enormous arched windows open up to a completely revamped 100 year-old room, featuring long exposed ceiling beams, whitewashed brick, dark slate walls and soft leather chairs.

But even with all that design swag, the main draw at Pearl's Southern Comfort is still the food. For starters, there's the ace barbecue, but guests should hardly stop there. Try the enormous double cut pork chop, grilled to supple perfection and paired with "dirty" farro salad, Cajun slaw and pork jus. Another staple, the Louisiana jambalaya, is served decadently dark and spicy, brimming with tender chicken, Andouille sausage and Crystal hot sauce.

▪ 5352 N. Broadway (bet. Balmoral & Berwyn Aves.)
Ⓜ Berwyn
✆ (773) 754-7419 — **WEB:** www.pearlschicago.com
▪ Lunch Sat – Sun Dinner nightly   **PRICE: $$**

PHO 777 ⦙❍

Vietnamese • Simple

MAP: E4

A market's worth of fresh ingredients allows Pho 777 to stand out in a neighborhood where Vietnamese restaurants—and their signature soup—seem to populate every storefront. Bottles of hot sauce, jars of fiery condiments and canisters of spoons and chopsticks clustered on each table make it easy for regulars to sit down and start slurping.

Add choices like meatballs, tendon, flank steak and tofu to the cardamom- ginger- and clove-spiced beef broth, which fills a vat large enough to sate a lumberjack-sized appetite. Then throw in jalapeños, Thai basil and mint to your liking. If you're not feeling like pho this time around, snack on spring rolls with house-made roasted peanut sauce; or a stack of lacy bánh xèo stuffed with pork, chili sauce and sprouts.

▨ 1063-65 W. Argyle St. (bet. Kenmore & Winthrop Aves.)
🚇 Argyle
✆ (773) 561-9909 — **WEB:** N/A
▨ Lunch & dinner Tue – Sun   PRICE: ⊜

PHO XE TANG - TANK NOODLE ⦙❍

Vietnamese • Simple

♿ BYO⟿   **MAP:** E4

A stone's throw from the Little Saigon EL, this simple corner spot keeps pho enthusiasts coming back for more. Communal cafeteria-style tables, crowded during prime meal times, are stocked with all the necessary funky and spicy condiments. Efficient service keeps the joint humming and lets the patrons focus on slurping.

Pho is the definitive draw here, and this fragrant, five-spiced, rice noodle- and beef-filled broth is accompanied by sprouts, lime wedges and plenty of basil. Other delights on the massive menu include shrimp- and pork-stuffed rice flour rolls with spicy and sour nuoc cham. Follow that with a fiery catfish soup simmered with an intriguing combination of okra, pineapple and crunchy bamboo shoots drizzled with garlic oil.

▨ 4953-55 N. Broadway (at Argyle St.)
🚇 Argyle
✆ (773) 878-2253 — **WEB:** www.tank-noodle.com
▨ Lunch & dinner Thu – Tue   PRICE: ⊜

RAS DASHEN

Ethiopian · Simple

MAP: E2

If you're lucky, grab a stool at one of the mossab tables to relish this Ethiopian kitchen's authentic cooking. Walls splashed with rust-orange and rattan chairs further elevate the faithful appeal, while a bar pouring honey wine and African beers keeps the local community happy.

Collective trays with delicacies speed out of the kitchen, so those who wish to immerse themselves in this nation's culinary culture should begin—on a light note—with Zenash's salad tossing chickpeas and crispy shallots with a touch of vinegar and tons of toasty spices. Gored gored highlights brisket marinated with awaze; and yebeg alicha is an aromatic lamb stew complete with spicy veggies. Sides of spongy and tart injera are ideal for cooling the palate from the creeping heat.

5846 N. Broadway (bet. Ardmore & Thorndale Aves.)

Thorndale

(773) 506-9601 — **WEB:** www.rasdashenchicago.com

Lunch & dinner Wed – Mon

PRICE: $$

SABRI NIHARI 😋

Indian · Family

MAP: C1

Sabri Nihari outshines the restaurant competition on this crowded stretch of West Devon Avenue. Make your way inside the expansive and massively posh Indo-Pakistani spot, where crystal chandeliers make gold-hued walls gleam more brightly.

As with many South Asian restaurants, vegetarian dishes abound—but that's only the beginning of the diverse menu. Whole okra pods add a grassy, peppery bite to beefy bhindi gosht, and delightful chicken charga, an entire spatchcocked bird marinated in yogurt and lime, is rubbed generously with spices before crisping up in the deep fryer. No alcohol is served in deference to many of the abstaining clientele, but you won't miss it. Buttery naan and creamy lassi with homemade yogurt help to balance out the spice-fest.

2500-2502 W. Devon Ave. (at Campbell Ave.)

(773) 465-3272 — **WEB:** www.sabrinihari.com

Lunch & dinner daily

PRICE: 🍜

SAN SOO GAB SAN 🐶

Korean • Family

MAP: C4

Tucked into a tiny strip mall in the West Edgewater-Upper Andersonville area, San Soo Gab San has generated quite a buzz among serious Korean food fans. Inside, you'll find a warm, welcoming space with large tabletop grills to cook your own meats.

Most excitingly, the authentic, traditional dishes turned out of the kitchen don't bow or cater to Western sensibilities—to wit, an incredibly flavorful bowl of piping hot goat meat soup arrives with wild sesame leaves and a flutter of seeds. Among the many popular casseroles and stews, don't miss the beoseot doenjang jjigae, chockablock with tender tofu, savory mushrooms, beef and veggies. The delicious barbecue is perfect for a group feast or those looking to have some fun with their food.

- 5247 N. Western Ave. (at Berwyn Ave.)
- Western (Brown)
- (773) 334-1589 — **WEB:** www.ssgsbbq.com
- Lunch & dinner daily   PRICE: $$

TASTE OF PERU 🍴

Peruvian • Simple

BYO   **MAP:** D1

Tucked inside a strip mall and entirely plain-Jane in appearance, foodies trek to this fave for a formidable meal of authentic dishes. The owner is chatty and tunes groovy, all of which make for a wonderful precursor to such peppery items as aji de gallina (shredded chicken in a walnut sauce, enriched with parmesan) or chupe de camarones (a hot, spicy, bright bowl of shrimp and rice). This is not the place for a pisco sour, but feels like Sundays con la familia where papa a la huancaina doused in amarillo chile, and arroz chaufa with veggies and beef jerky-like strips are merely some of the items on offer.

It's worth noting though that while the food is decidedly traditional, mysteriously there's no pork to be found anywhere on the menu.

- 6545 N. Clark St. (bet. Albion & Arthur Aves.)
- (773) 381-4540 — **WEB:** www.tasteofperu.com
- Lunch & dinner daily   PRICE: 🍲

VINCENT
Belgian • Bistro

MAP: E3

Go Dutch at Vincent, where innovative yet approachable cooking meets a tried-and-true European bistro menu, boasting enough cheese to satisfy even the pickiest turophile. Adding to the romance, high-top marble tables and brocade-papered walls make for a warm, intimate ambience that's accented by tall votive candles.

Got an appetite? An overflowing pot of P.E.I. mussels is a decadent meal on its own, brimming with bits of pork belly, chilies, scallions and cilantro, accompanied by a big bowl of traditional frites with mayonnaise. Basil and lemon balsam perk up risotto with charred purple cauliflower and braised fennel. Also, you'll want to hold on to your fork for slices of lemon butter cake with Chantilly cream and blueberry compote.

- 1475 W. Balmoral Ave. (bet. Clark St. & Glenwood Ave.)
- Berwyn
- (773) 334-7168 — **WEB:** www.vincentchicago.com
- Lunch Sun Dinner Tue – Sun   **PRICE: $$**

THE WARBLER
American • Chic

MAP: C5

All neighborhood restaurants should aspire to be more like The Warbler. This latest venture from the team behind gather is located just next door, and features a dining room that is far more sleek and contemporary than you might expect. Yet it remains as comfy as ever, helping it become an instant staple.

The playful cooking clearly shows effort as seen in their house-made pastas and artistic plating, but is always accessible and appealing. Chitarra twirled around blistered tomatoes in a buttery garlic sauce with shrimp are not only delicious but reasonably priced. The menu is also full of American classics like wings, nachos and flatbreads, but save room for desserts—like a carrot cake drenched in so much toffee sauce, it may as well be called a pudding.

- 4535 N. Lincoln Ave. (bet. Sunnyside & Wilson Aves.)
- Western (Brown)
- (773) 681-0950 — **WEB:** www.thewarblerchicago.com
- Dinner nightly   **PRICE: $$**

BUCKTOWN & WICKER PARK

UKRANIAN VILLAGE · WEST TOWN

A CAVE OF COOL

Like many of the Windy City's neighborhoods, Bucktown and Wicker Park have seen their residents shift from waves of Polish immigrants and wealthy families who've erected stately mansions on Hoyne and Pierce avenues, to those young, hip crowds introducing modern taquerias and craft breweries to these streets. Still, the neighborhood knows how to retain its trendsetting rep, and continues to draw those who crave to be on the cutting edge of all things creative, contemporary, and culinary. Far from the internationally known boutiques along Magnificent Mile, indie shops and artisan producers of Milwaukee and Damen avenues offer one-of-a-kind treasures for all the five senses. Get a taste of Wicker Park's vast underground music scene at Reckless Records or at some of the city's largest music events, including the Wicker Park Fest, which is held each July and features no less than 28 bands. Likewise, the annual Green Music Fest draws every eco-minded resident

around. Snap up funky home accessories and original works at flea market-chic Penguin Foot Pottery, or wear art on your sleeve by designing your own tee at the appropriately named T-shirt Deli.

HOT DOGS AND HAUTE TREATS

It's a well-known saying that you don't want to know how the sausage is made, but the person who coined this phrase clearly never tasted the bounty from **Vienna Beef Factory**. Their popular workshop tour leaves visitors yearning for a 1/3-pound Mike Ditka Polish sausage at the café, or even a make-your-own-Chicago-dog kit with celery salt, sport peppers, and electric-green pickle relish from the gift shop. For more Eastern European fun, **Rich's Deli** is Ukrainian Village's go-to market for copious cuts of smoked pork as well as kabanosy, pasztet, Polish vodka, and Slavic mustard among other terrific stuff.

Unlike many local emporiums in town, the staff here is fluent in English, so don't be afraid to make your inquiries. All other lingering questions on meat may be answered after talking with husband-and-wife team, Rob and Allie Levitt, the brains (and stomachs) behind Noble Square's **The Butcher & Larder**. Combining the growing interest in whole animal butchery and a desire to support local farmers, the Levitts showcase sausages, terrines, and house-cured bacon, while also conducting demos on how to break down a side of beef. If God is indeed in the details, then marketplace extraordinaire, **Goddess & Grocer**, brings to life this turn of phrase. While its vast selection of items may be the stuff of dreams among

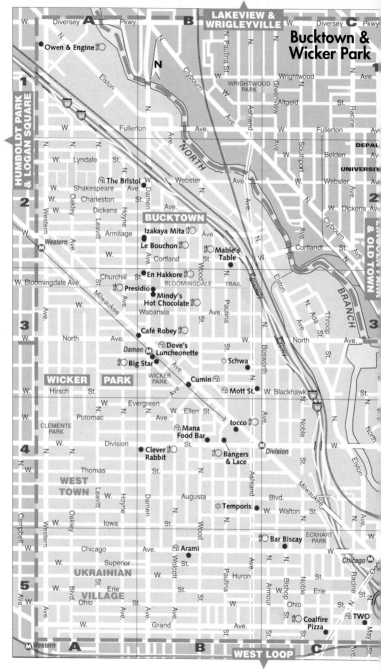

Bucktown & Wicker Park

W. Diversey A Pkwy.
B
W. Diversey C Pkwy.

● Owen & Engine ‖○

N

Clybourn

N. Paulina St.

WRIGHTWOOD PARK

Wrightwood

Greenview

Altgeld

Ave.

St.

Racine

Elston

Ave.

N.

NORTH

W. Fullerton

Ave.

Ashland

W. Fullerton

Av

Southport

DEPA

Belden

Av

UNIVERSI

W. Lyndale St.

W. Webster

Ave.

W. Webster

N.

Clybourn

St.

W. Dickens Av

W. Shakespeare Ave.

(亞) The Bristol ‖○

Damen

W.

W. Oakley Charleston St.

W. Dickens Ave.

W. Dickens Av

Hoyne

W. Leavitt Armitage

BUCKTOWN

Izakaya Mita ‖○

Ave.

Cortlandt

St.

& OLD TOWN

Western

Ave.

Le Bouchon ‖○

Milwaukee

Ave.

‖○ Mable's Table

N.

Wood

St.

Elston

Clybourn

BRANCH

W. Bloomingdale Ave.

Churchill St.

● En Hakkore ‖○

BLOOMINGDALE TRAIL

Ada St.

Throop

N.

Damen

‖○ Presidio ●

Mindy's

Hot Chocolate ‖○

Ramsay

N.

Bosworth

St.

St.

W. Wabansia

Ave.

Paulina

W. North

Ave.

● Café Robey ‖○

N.

North

Ave.

N.

St.

W. Blackhawk

Damen M Dove's
Luncheonette

Ave.

St.

N.

‖○ Big Star ●

WICKER PARK

❀ Schwa

W. Hirsch St.

Cumin (亞)

(亞) Mott St. ●

N.

Noble

St.

Milwaukee

W. Evergreen

Ave.

W. Ellen St.

CLEMENTE PARK

N.

W. Potomac

tocco ‖○ ●

(亞) Mana
Food Bar ●

W. Division

St.

‖○ Bangers
& Lace ●

M Division

Ashland

St.

W.

● Clever
Rabbit

Elston

Milwaukee

WEST TOWN

W. Thomas

St.

Leavitt

W. Augusta

Blvd.

Hoyne

N.

Damen

❀ Temporis ●

W. Walton St.

St.

Wood

W. Iowa

St.

Ave.

Western

Campbell

ECKHART PARK

W. Chicago

(亞) Arami

‖○ Bar Biscay ●

Ave.

St.

Wolcott

Chicago M

Racine

W. Superior

St.

Paulina

Huron

St.

St.

UKRAINIAN

W. Erie

St.

VILLAGE

Bishop

Noble

W. Erie

St.

Armour

Ave.

Western

Blvd.

W. Ohio

St.

Ave.

Ave.

Ave.

W. Ohio

St.

‖○ Coalfire
Pizza ●

(亞) TWO

W. Grand

Ave.

May St.

M Western A

B

C

snooty gourmands and top chefs, even novices can be found here, stocking up on soups, salads, and chili—better than what Mom used to make back in the day. They also cater, so go ahead and pretend like you crafted those delicate dinner party hors d'oeuvres all on your own!

SUGAR RUSH

A spectrum of hand-crafted goodies make this region a rewarding destination for anyone addicted to sweet. For nearly a century, family-run **Margie's Candies** has been hand-dipping its chocolate bonbons and serving towering scoops of homemade ice cream to those Logan Square denizens and dons (including Al Capone, that old softy). Equally retro in attitude, the lip-smacking seasonal slices and small-town vibe of **Hoosier Mama Pie Company** brings old-timey charm to this stretch of Chicago Avenue. From tiered wedding cakes to replicas of Wrigley Field recreated in batter and frosting, a tempting selection of desserts is displayed in the window at **Alliance Bakery** and would make even Willy Wonka green with envy. But, if you're looking for something a little less traditional, unusual combinations are the norm at **Black Dog Gelato**, where goat cheese, cashew, and caramel come together for a uniquely rich scoop.

SUDS AND SPUDS

The craft beer movement has been brewing in Chicagoland for some time now, where

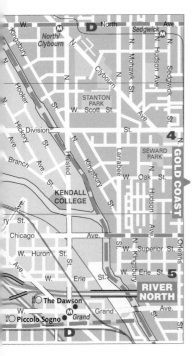

lovers of quality suds and superlative bar snacks find an impressive listing of both in Bucktown and Wicker Park. Regulars at Logan Square's **Revolution Brewing** snack on bacon-fat popcorn and sweet potato cakes while sipping on the in-house Double Fist Pale Ale or Anti-Hero IPA. This holy union between food and beer is always reaching epic heights at **Piece Brewery & Pizzeria**, which not only serves up one of Chicagoland's most popular hand-tossed pizzas but also produces a roster of award-winning beers to accompany its crusty New Haven-style pies. And, for a master class on the wide and wonderful world of craft brews, the noted beer school at Wicker Park's **Map Room** gives students a greater appreciation for the art—though a self-taught tour of the bar's worldwide selection is quite educational and perhaps more enjoyable?

THE LUSH LIFE

However, if south-of-the-border eats are what you need, then head on over to **Taco & Burrito Express #3**. This fast, family-run, and cash-only spot doles out delicious al pastor tacos until the party winds down—at 11:00 P.M. For those who prefer their treats brought to them in creative ice cream and frozen yogurt flavors, **Jeni's Splendid Ice Creams** in Wicker Park is yet another fixture here that brings the community together. Crowds of another sort covene at all

hours at **Emporium Arcade Bar** where rows of video games and pinball machines from the 1980s bring back memories for those who grew up hitting the arcade. And this of course becomes even more fun when paired with a craft beer or whiskey shot.

KITCHEN SKILLS

Meals at **The Dining Room at Kendall College** let you brag about knowing future Michelin-starred chefs before they've hit it big. As one of Chicago's premier culinary institutions, this college gives its chef trainees real-world guidance by way of elegant lunch and dinner service. Floor-to-ceiling windows overlook the professional kitchen, where instructors can be seen helping students fine-tune their fine dining skills. Reservations are required, but the experience is a must for home cooks looking to be inspired. For a more hands-on affair, classes at **Cooking Fools** let aspiring Food Network stars hone their knife skills

or prepare a batch of tamales from scratch. Feeling the need to flaunt your culinary credentials over a dinner party at home? Simply swing by the cash-only **Wicker Park & Bucktown Farmer's Market** and stock your pantry with an impressive fleet of fresh produce, artisanal cheeses, and much, much more. Afterwards, you can always peruse the shelves of **Olivia's Market** for painstakingly sourced specialty items, as well as a massive wine and beer selection. Then drop by **LocalFolks Foods**, a family-run enterprise whose chief mission is to develop natural gourmet condiments (mustard and hot sauce anyone?) for slathering over hearty burgers or dogs. You may also purchase these same delightful treats from the lauded **Green Grocer** and make your next cookout the envy of everyone on the block. Finally feel ready to grow your own vegetables? Sign up for a plot at **Frankie Machine Community Garden** and see if you've got a green thumb!

ARAMI 🏵

Japanese • *Contemporary décor*

🍶 ♿   **MAP:** B5

Come to this bamboo-clad izakaya, with its comfortable sushi bar and soaring skylights, for impressively rendered small plates and specialty cocktails featuring Japanese spirits. The night's tsukemono can reveal spicy okra, crisp hearts of palm and sweet burdock root. The nigiri selection might showcase New Zealand King salmon topped with pickled wasabi root. The robata produces grilled maitakes with Japanese sea salt and black garlic purée; and gani korroke, a crunchy, creamy crab croquette, is plated with togarashi-spiked mayonnaise.

Don't turn down the all-ice cream dessert menu, which includes enticing flavors like coconut-cinnamon-banana. It comes nestled in granola-like bits of miso-graham cracker crumble for a finish as sweet as it is unique.

▧ 1829 W. Chicago Ave. (bet. Wolcott Ave & Wood St.)
🚇 Division
✆ (312) 243-1535 — **WEB:** www.aramichicago.com
▧ Dinner nightly   **PRICE:** $$

BANGERS & LACE 🍴

Gastropub • *Tavern*

🍺 ♿ 🛋   **MAP:** B4

Despite the frilly connotations, this sausage-and-beer mecca's name refers not to doilies, but to the delicate layers of foam that remain in the glass after your craft brew has been quaffed. You'll also have plenty of opportunity to study the lace curtains as you plow through their extensive draft beer menu, noted on blackboards in the comfortably worn-in front bar room.

Decadent foie gras corn dogs (actually French garlic sausage wrapped with soft-sweet brioche cornbread) and veal brats with melted Gouda elevate the humble sausage; while a slew of sandwiches suit simpler tastes. Grilled cheese gilds the lily with taleggio, raclette, and Irish cheddar; and house-made chips drizzled with truffle oil and malt vinegar are more than a bar snack.

▧ 1670 W. Division St. (at Paulina St.)
🚇 Damen (Blue)
✆ (773) 252-6499 — **WEB:** www.bangersandlacechicago.com
▧ Lunch Sat – Sun Dinner nightly   **PRICE:** $$

BAR BISCAY ¶O

Basque • *Trendy*

&

MAP: C5

This bright and beautiful addition to the Noble Square scene arrives courtesy of the owners behind the popular mfk. Inside, the music can get loud, and the crowd even louder, but the bright lights and upbeat vibe is contagious, so have a few glasses of that vermouth (on tap!) and lean into it. You've landed at one of the trendiest places in town.

The dinner menu is laid out in groups like "from vegetables" or "from the sea." The latter might unveil classic Basque dishes like a conserva of anchovies tossed with fennel, red onion and excellent olive oil; or even chewy razor clams bathed with a rich, herbaceous and lemony sauce. For dessert, a gargantuan strawberry crêpe tucked with quince and lemon-Neufchatel, has sweet addicts rightfully swooning.

- 1450 W. Chicago Ave. (bet. Bishop St. & Greenview Ave.)
- Chicago (Blue)
- (312) 455-8900 — **WEB:** www.barbiscay.com
- Dinner nightly

PRICE: $$

BIG STAR ¶O

Mexican • *Simple*

MAP: B3

Bucktown's favorite taqueria has all the fixings for a fiesta. Craft beers, custom-bottled Bourbons and pitchers of margaritas wash down the affordable abundance. And, despite the grungy décor, the vibe is as intoxicating as the aroma of the taco de chorizo verde. The patio is even more of a party, and sun-starved Chicagoans can be spotted out there soon after the groundhog has (or hasn't) seen his shadow.

Tacos are served individually, thus allowing ample opportunity to graze on the likes of the pollo pibil—achiote- and citrus-marinated chicken thighs steamed in banana leaves, topped with pickled onion slices and cilantro. Save room for the salsa de frijole con queso, a crock of pinto bean dip accompanied by lime salt-sprinkled tortilla chips.

- 1531 N. Damen Ave. (bet. Milwaukee & Wicker Park Aves.)
- Damen (Blue)
- (773) 235-4039 — **WEB:** www.bigstarchicago.com
- Lunch & dinner daily

PRICE: ⊜⊜

THE BRISTOL

American • Neighborhood

MAP: B2

Get to know your neighbors a little better at this dim, bustling haunt boasting seasonal American fare with a Mediterranean twist. Regulars sit shoulder-to-shoulder at the concrete bar, squinting under filament bulbs to see the constantly changing menu's latest additions on chalkboards throughout the room.

Start with a Moscow Mule in a frosty copper mug to go with your head-on prawns a la plancha with anchovy butter and tarragon, or smoked whitefish dip with horseradish and saltines. Large plates sing with comfort, especially the Amish half-chicken with mustard-dill spaetzle and chicken jus.

Weekend brunch is mighty popular, whether for the hangover-curing noodle bowl or plump cinnamon rolls. Homemade nutter butters remain an iconic finale.

- 2152 N. Damen Ave. (bet. Shakespeare & Webster Aves.)
- Western (Blue)
- (773) 862-5555 — **WEB:** www.thebristolchicago.com
- Lunch Sat – Sun Dinner nightly   **PRICE: $$**

CAFE ROBEY

American • Chic

MAP: B3

Resting on one of the intersections of Chicago's famous six corners in Wicker Park, this stunning restaurant is nestled at the base of the chic Robey hotel. The room dazzles at every turn with its midcentury modern-meets-contemporary brasserie vibe, just as the kitchen turns out elegant reinterpretations of familiar dishes. Imagine the likes of butter-poached shrimp over tender escarole, or cod topped with a soft brioche, leek crust and sided by artichoke barigoule as well as crisp prosciutto ribbons. The terrific rhubarb clafoutis with a ginger-rhubarb sorbet is so good you won't want it to ever end. Brunch is available daily, so you'll no longer need to wait for the weekend.

Street views charm, but head to the rooftop for an even better vantage point.

- 1616 N. Milwaukee Ave. (at North Ave.)
- Damen (Blue)
- (872) 315-3084 — **WEB:** www.caferobey.com
- Lunch & dinner daily   **PRICE: $$$**

CLEVER RABBIT

American • Contemporary décor

On a crowded stretch of Division, Clever Rabbit pulls away from the pack thanks to its inventive menu and rustic-chic space, featuring a marble-topped bar, whitewashed brick walls and modern lighting. The professional staff is well versed on the vegetable-forward menu, so heed their counsel and begin with the mushroom and polenta terrine with walnuts and a pumpkin marmalade. Then dive into carrot dumplings or the pig ear (shaped) pasta with braised broccoli rabe and ricotta. Finesse and flavor reign in such items as the North African chicken seasoned with ras el hanout or tuna with compressed cucumber and puffed wild rice.

Go ahead and dangle that carrot cake. This triple-layer treat with a cream cheese filling and olive oil "jam" is the ultimate reward.

- 2015 W. Division St. (bet. Hoyne & Damen Aves.)
- Division (Blue)
- (773) 697-8711 — **WEB:** www.cleverrabbitchicago.com
- Lunch Sat – Sun Dinner nightly   PRICE: $$$

COALFIRE PIZZA

Pizza • Family

MAP: C5

Sure, you could come for a salad, but the focus here is on pizza—and yours should be, too. The dining room is cozy, showcasing an open kitchen where pie production is on full display for all to see. And in a playful bit of recycling, empty tomato sauce cans placed on each table become stands for sizzling pizzas churned straight from the 800-degree coal-fired oven.

This hot spot has its ratio down to a fine art and knows not to burden its thin and crispy crust that's blackened and blistered in all the right places. The mortadella is a delight, with chopped garlic and gossamer slices of peppercorn-flecked sausage. But if you wish to go your own way, build the perfect pie with toppings that run the gamut from decadent Gorgonzola to tangy goat cheese.

- 1321 W. Grand Ave. (bet. Ada & Elizabeth Sts.)
- Chicago (Blue)
- (312) 226-2625 — **WEB:** www.coalfirechicago.com
- Lunch Fri – Sun Dinner Tue – Sun   PRICE: ⊕⊕

CUMIN 🄰
Indian • *Neighborhood*

♿

MAP: B3

This proudly run blend of Nepalese and Indian eats sits among a plethora of bars, coffee shops and vintage stores in boho-centric Bucktown. While fans of the sub-continent love Cumin for its clean and modern surrounds, linen-lined tables struggle to contain the myriad plates that pile up during its ubiquitous lunch buffet.

Paintings of mountain scenes decorate crimson-red walls and prep diners for an authentic range of flavorful food hailing from the Himalayan frontier. Get gnawing on namche sekuwa—tandoori goat flecked with spices and paired with crunchy green peppers. Then soak up pieces of buttery naan in a hearty vegetarian stew (aalu tama bodi) combining potatoes, bamboo shoots and black-eyed peas. Cool things down with sweet and milky mango kulfi.

◾ 1414 N. Milwaukee Ave. (bet. Evergreen & Wolcott Aves.)
◾ Damen (Blue)
☎ (773) 342-1414 — **WEB:** www.cumin-chicago.com
◾ Lunch Tue – Sun Dinner nightly **PRICE:** 💰💰

THE DAWSON 🍴
Gastropub • *Trendy*

🍸 ♿ ⛱ 🖥 🛋 🧾

MAP: D5

The Dawson has everything you can ask for in a gastropub—a convivial vibe, clever bites and great libations. The Surfer Rosa for instance (with tequila, mezcal, blood orange and chilies) serves to loosen up diners jonesing for big flavors. Inside, globe lights shine like beacons through the façade's lofty windows. And, a wraparound bar attracts spirited guests like moths to a flame. A communal table and open kitchen with counter offer multiple opportunities for meeting, greeting and eating.

When hunger strikes, caramelized onion sabayon, potato confit and garlicky pea shoots add depth to Arctic char. And lest you forget dessert, Bourbon-pecan bread pudding with flash-frozen vanilla cream and sea salt-butterscotch sauce, is meant for sharing—or not.

◾ 730 W. Grand Ave. (at Halsted St.)
◾ Grand (Blue)
☎ (312) 243-8955 — **WEB:** www.the-dawson.com
◾ Lunch Sat – Sun Dinner nightly **PRICE:** $$

DOVE'S LUNCHEONETTE
American · Neighborhood

MAP: B3

With a chill, throwback vibe, all-day breakfast and a drink list with more than 70 labels of agave spirits, this One Off Hospitality roadhouse is a Wicker Park hipster's dream come true. To drive the point home, the diner features wood-paneled walls, counter seating, a record player spinning the blues and of course, Tex-Mex fare listed on a wall-mounted letter board. The daily special may be a blueberry quinoa pancake, while savory favorites include crunchy buttermilk fried chicken with chorizo verde gravy or the farmer's cheese-stuffed Anaheim chile relleno, served in a pool of tomato-serrano sauce with pasilla chiles and pickled chayote slices.

Pies from Hoosier Mama Pie Co. are a grand finale; try the lemony Atlantic Beach with a saltine crust.

■ 1545 N. Damen Ave. (bet. Milwaukee & Pierce Aves.)
▥ Damen (Blue)
☏ (773) 645-4060 — **WEB:** www.doveschicago.com
■ Lunch & dinner daily

PRICE: $$

EN HAKKORE
Korean · Simple

MAP: B3

Healthy doesn't have to be humdrum. This simple little Korean eatery, run by a husband-and-wife team and decorated with more than a hint of whimsy, specializes in big bowls of bibimbap. You choose your rice and protein, be it pork or barbecue beef, decide on the heat level and then dive straight in—up to 16 different vegetables are used and they're as tasty as they are colorful. Also worth trying are the steamed mandoo (pork dumplings) and the curiously addictive tacos made with paratha.

Simply place your order at the counter, grab a plastic fork and, if you're with friends, commandeer the large communal table. There's no alcohol (and it's not BYOB) so instead take advantage of an invigorating soft drink from the fridge. You'll feel so virtuous.

■ 1840 N. Damen Ave. (bet. Churchill & Moffat Sts.)
▥ Damen (Blue)
☏ (773) 772-9880 — **WEB:** N/A
■ Lunch & dinner Mon – Sat

PRICE: ⊜

IZAKAYA MITA ❧

Japanese • Simple

MAP: B2

This Bucktown favorite is a family-run tavern worth seeking out for its homespun take on izakaya eats and gracious hospitality.

Start with single-serve sake in a jar so cute you'll want to smuggle it home, or a cocktail inspired by Japanese literature (the Norwegian Wood, a delicious interpretation of the Haruki Murakami novel blends whiskey, Luxardo, sweet vermouth and orange bitters). The array of small plates brims with creativity and flavor: tsukune are coarseground, delightfully chewy and achieve a mouthwateringly charred exterior from having been grilled over bincho-tan; while tako-yaki are as delicious as any found on a Tokyo street cart. Korroke, a pankocrusted potato croquette, comes with tonkatsu sauce for delicious dunking.

- 1960 N. Damen Ave. (at Armitage Ave.)
- Western (Blue)
- (773) 799-8677 — **WEB:** www.izakayamita.com
- Lunch Sat – Sun Dinner nightly

PRICE: ❧❧

LE BOUCHON ❧

French • Bistro

MAP: B2

Pressed-tin ceilings? Check. Brick-and-Dijon color scheme? Of course. Le Bouchon proffers the quintessential bistro experience, where straightforward French cooking never goes out of style and the regulars keep returning for more. The informal atmosphere gets convivially raucous as the night goes on with thirsty and hungry hordes lining the bar and petite dining room.

Over in the kitchen, familiar and approachable favorites rule the menu: soupe à l'oignon, wearing its traditional topper of broiled Gruyère on a moist crouton, oozes and bubbles over the sides of a ramekin. And an ample fillet of saumon poché napped in beurre blanc is the very essence of simplicity.

A lunch prix-fixe keeps the wallet light but belly full.

- 1958 N. Damen Ave. (at Armitage Ave.)
- Damen (Blue)
- (773) 862-6600 — **WEB:** www.lebouchonofchicago.com
- Lunch & dinner Mon – Sat

PRICE: $$

MABLE'S TABLE
American • Neighborhood

MAP: B2

It's Mother's Day every day at Mable's Table, where Chef/owner Anthony Reyes pays homage to his own mamá with a spectrum of classic comfort food. This "table" is big on the cozy factor—just one of the reasons you'll find everyone here, from couples and children to suits closing deals over meals.

The menu may be concise but dishes leave a lasting impression. Whitefish is prepared simply with a crispy pan-sear and finished with a light Meyer lemon-butter sauce. Then move on to the pièce de résistance—porchetta bollio loaded with juicy, roast pork full of layers of sweet fat, dill pickles and cheese. It is quite simply heaven on a roll, with a side of fries, natch. For a balanced feast, finish with a wonderfully tart slice of key lime pie.

1655 W. Cortland St. (bet. Paulina St. & Marshfield Ave.)

(773) 904-7433 — **WEB:** www.mablestable.com

Lunch & dinner daily

PRICE: $$

MANA FOOD BAR
Vegetarian • Minimalist

MAP: B4

Mana, whose name translates to "The life force coursing through nature," is a good place to get your mojo back. And the back is where you'll need to go, since their front space is now the domain of Anaba Handroll Bar.

Though welcoming to vegans, gluten-free diners and anyone else who's looking for a nutrient boost, Mana is not just health food: the small space also offers a full bar with sake cocktails, smoothies and freshly squeezed juices. The restaurant may be a tiny one, but its diverse menu of vegetarian dishes is big on taste—and spice. Korean bibimbap mixes a roster of vegetables like pea pods, roasted carrots and pickled daikon with a fresh sunny side-up egg; while horseradish and cracked black pepper sneak into macaroni and cheese.

1742 W. Division St. (bet. Paulina & Wood Sts.)

Division

(773) 342-1742 — **WEB:** www.manafoodbar.com

Lunch Sat Dinner nightly

PRICE: $$

MINDY'S HOT CHOCOLATE

American • Friendly

MAP: B3

Bucktown wouldn't be the same without this sweet spot run by pastry chef extraordinaire, Mindy Segal. Diners walk past decadent hot chocolate mix and cookies on display before hitting an industrial-chic space fitted with sleek dark wood, caramel-brown walls and chocolate-toned leather banquettes.

Decadent chocolate is the name of the game, though diners will also discover delicious savory items. Try the roasted tomato soup, garnished with green onion slivers; or the BLT with pesto-seasoned aïoli, heirloom tomato, avocado and thick, crispy maple-cayenne bacon. An affogato—a scoop of coffee-cocoa nib ice cream paired with the chef's namesake hot chocolate—makes for the perfect finale.

Get your fix outside Bucktown at the outpost in Revival Food Hall.

🔳 1747 N. Damen Ave. (bet. St. Paul Ave. & Willow St.)
🔳 Damen (Blue)
✆ (773) 489-1747 — **WEB:** www.hotchocolatechicago.com
🔳 Lunch Wed – Sun Dinner Tue – Sun   **PRICE: $$**

MOTT ST. ☺

Fusion • Trendy

MAP: B3

New Yorkers know Mott St. as the bustling artery in the heart of Chinatown, but to Chicagoans the name connotes something off the beaten path. Inside the low-slung, stand-alone red structure, a chicken wire-caged pantry is stocked with jars of red pepper, black vinegar and other pungent edibles—all of which appear again in the food on your plate.

Offerings at this hip haven crisscross the globe, melding diverse ingredients for an utterly unique dining experience. Shredded kohlrabi substitutes green papaya for a Thai-inspired salad tossed with candied shrimp, poached chicken and plenty of fresh herbs. Stuffed cabbage bears a Korean accent with tender chunks of slow-braised pork, tangy Napa cabbage kimchi and crunchy sticky rice.

🔳 1401 N. Ashland Ave. (at Blackhawk St.)
🔳 Division
✆ (773) 687-9977 — **WEB:** www.mottstreetchicago.com
🔳 Lunch Sun Dinner Tue – Sat   **PRICE: $$**

OWEN & ENGINE
Gastropub • Tavern

MAP: A1

Owen & Engine's charm extends from its glossy black façade into its warm polished wood interior and all the way to the second-floor dining room that sees action into the wee hours. Brocade wallpaper, gas lights and studded leather club chairs lend a Victorian feel. A frequently changing draft list always features a few selections pulled from a beer cask (or "engine").

British-inspired gastropub grub matches the impressive roster of brews and Pimm's cups. Bar nibbles like mustard-glazed soft pretzels with Welsh rarebit for dipping; or peanuts tossed in sriracha, Worcestershire and brown sugar cater to the snacking sort. Hearty entrées like bangers and mash combine house-made Slagel Family Farm's pork sausage and potatoes smothered in onion gravy.

2700 N. Western Ave. (at Schubert Ave.)
(773) 235-2930 — **WEB:** www.owenengine.com
Lunch Sat – Sun Dinner nightly   **PRICE: $$**

PICCOLO SOGNO
Italian • Trattoria

MAP: D5

In-the-know locals craving mouthwatering Italian food head to this swanky spot, usually packed with a dressy crowd. Inside, they are welcomed by a palette of rich, cool hues, crystal-beaded light fixtures that hang overhead and an open kitchen boasting a wood-burning oven.

Piccolo Sogno's rustic yet refined menu offers traditional dishes with a twist. A version of the ubiquitous beet salad (both red and golden) is elevated here by shaved fennel, a drizzle of bright citrus oil and a dollop of creamy, lush buffalo milk ricotta. If you need further encouragement, let us recommend the rabbit. Braised in a white wine sauce redolent of rosemary and lemon, the tender meat is served with wilted escarole and porridge-like semolina pudding.

464 N. Halsted St. (at Milwaukee Ave.)
Grand (Blue)
(312) 421-0077 — **WEB:** www.piccolosognorestaurant.com
Lunch Mon – Fri Dinner nightly   **PRICE: $$**

PRESIDIO
Contemporary · Chic

MAP: B3

With its gorgeous bar, rustic brick walls and flickering candles, Presidio will have you smitten upon entrance, but this sleeper is as long on substance as it is on looks. Chef Nicole Bayani transports diners to northern California by way of simple, yet sensational and seasonally informed dishes. A salad of butter lettuce with clusters of seaweed nut crunch in a carrot-ginger dressing, for instance, proves that simplicity is the best policy. Thick ribbons of pappardelle are then tossed with melted leeks, baby kale, peas and parmesan to portray the essence of California cooking—at its finest—just as cod in a thick, smoky tomato broth shows serious skill.

Buttermilk-crème fraîche panna cotta with strawberry-rhubarb jam is spot on—and the ideal finale.

- 1749 N. Damen (at Willow St.)
- Damen (Blue)
- (773) 697-3315 — **WEB:** www.presidiochicago.com
- Lunch Sun Dinner nightly   **PRICE: $$$**

TOCCO
Italian · Contemporary décor

MAP: B4

Are we in Milan or Wicker Park? Tocco brings haute design to the dining table with such upscale textural touches as polished resin, faux ostrich skin and bubblegum-pink accents in this sleek black-and-white space. Don your catwalk best before visiting: a fashion-centric display near a long communal table hints at the chichi theme present throughout.

The décor is cutting-edge, but the menu respects and returns to Italian standbys. Gnocco fritto, a doughy pillow served with charcuterie, is irresistible to even the most willowy fashionistas; while cracker-crisp artisan pizzas from wood-burning ovens are equally pleasing. Traditional involtini di pollo, pounded thin and rolled around prosciutto, get a hit of brightness from lemon and white wine sauce.

- 1266 N. Milwaukee Ave. (bet. Ashland Ave. & Paulina St.)
- Division
- (773) 687-8895 — **WEB:** www.toccochicago.com
- Dinner Tue – Sun   **PRICE: $$**

SCHWA ✿
Contemporary · Trendy

BYO⊐

MAP: B3

There comes a point when pared-down style jumps from being easy-to-miss and becomes hard-to-forget. When a utilitarian and self-consciously bare-bones interior becomes attractively modern and industrial. When a lack of any FOH staff makes the service seem playfully all-hands-on-deck. The explicit rap music playing in the background reflects the deeply talented chefs' ethos, going well beyond laissez-faire to reach the point of "we don't give a damn." You probably won't either once you taste the food—not every dish on their unabashedly creative menu works, but when it does, the results are sublime.

The extensive nightly tasting has no formal progression to speak of, but the team is chatty and ready to describe each item, sometimes from over their shoulder by another table.

Dinner might reveal homemade rolled pappardelle, laced with beurre monté and paired with peas, ramp purée, nasturtium and delightful uni bubbles; or a generous lobe of poached foie gras, topped with hazelnut, cocoa nib and brioche croutons, delicately laid over trumpet mushrooms and mango gel. For the finale, tender mackerel finds elevated company with hijiki slivers and custard, miso butter and spicy radish kimchi.

▨ 1466 N. Ashland Ave. (at Le Moyne St.)

▣ Division

℘ (773) 252-1466 — **WEB:** www.schwarestaurant.com

▨ Dinner Tue – Sat

PRICE: $$$$

TEMPORIS ✿
Contemporary • Elegant

&

Though this veritable jewel box deserves to have its name trumpeted in the streets, it is the epitome of serenity, sophistication and subtlety. With fewer than two-dozen seats, the space feels intimate, as if the whole show has been crafted for your benefit. Co-chefs Sam Plotnick and Don Young worked together at Les Nomades, and here at Temporis they continue to flaunt their supreme talent and collaboration. Each dish is a personal expression of their passion, vision and a clear representation of their highly intellectualized approach to cooking.

Custom tables featuring hydroponic sprouts that become part of your meal can also be found cradling such delicacies as escargot with a fermented sour cherry tomato. This then sets you on a course where you'll be surprised and delighted at every turn. Salmon in an uni broth; capellini with lobster morsels; a paper-thin biscuit with cured Mangalista pork—it's a culinary show of one intoxicating dish after the next. Ruby-red venison in a Madeira reduction is the stuff of dreams and may be tailed by decadent foie gras ice cream.

A chocolate tart is poured, then solidifies around a passion fruit-filled globe for a particularly dramatic final bow.

■ 933 N. Ashland Ave. (at Walton St.)
🚇 Division
✆ (773) 697-4961 — **WEB:** www.temporischicago.com
■ Dinner Tue – Sat   PRICE: $$$$

TWO

American • Neighborhood

MAP: C5

TWO is an urban interpretation of a Midwest tavern that was set up by two owners, features second-hand furnishings, and has an address whose last digit is—you guessed it—the number two. Beyond the vintage Toledo scales, find a reclaimed wood-paneled space dressed with antique meat cleavers, quaint ceiling fans and large barn doors.

This is a perfect lead into the farm-to-fork cuisine being whipped up in the open kitchen (the banquette across from it affords the best view). Start with classic Southern pimento cheese served in a miniature Mason jar alongside freshly grilled bread. Elegant small plates include pan-seared and spice-dusted halibut with fava beans and oyster mushrooms. On the sweet front, homemade puppy chow is chilled, crisp and delicious.

- 1132 W. Grand Ave. (at May St.)
- Chicago (Blue)
- (312) 624-8363 — **WEB:** www.113two.com
- Dinner Tue – Sun

PRICE: $$

Look for our symbol 🍇
spotlighting restaurants
with a notable wine list.

CHINATOWN & SOUTH

For years, the Red Line was the only true link between Chinatown and the South Loop. They may be neighbors geographically, but continue to remain distinct opposites in the culinary, architectural, and demographic spheres. Recent development on both sides of the line has brought the two worlds closer together, combining old and new flavors that make them irresistible to Chicago food lovers. The Great Chicago Fire spared many of the South Loop's buildings, making this architecture some of the oldest in the city. Residential palaces like the Glessner House and Clark House are now open for tours, but a quick walk along Prairie Avenue gives a self-guided view of marvelous mansions. Further north, those massive former lofts along Printers Row have been converted into condos, hotels, bookstores, and restaurants, as has the landmark Dearborn Station—the oldest train depot in Chicago.

SUN-UP TO SUNDOWN

The South Loop has the breakfast scene covered—quite literally—with dishes piled-high at casual neighborhood spots. Sop up a "South of the Border Benny" adorned with chorizo, or any number of egg favorites including frittata and French toast at **Yolk**, located on the southern end of Grant Park. The aptly named **Chicago Waffles** smothers

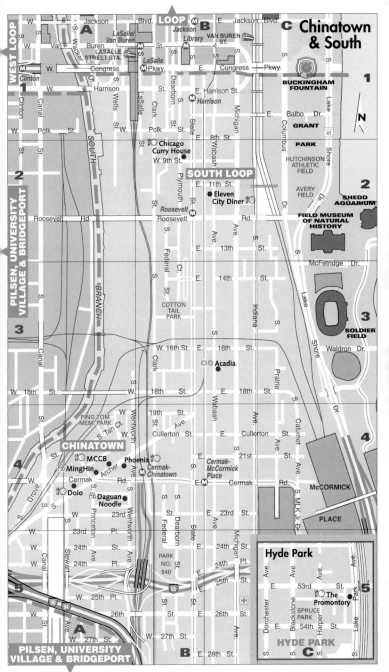

Chinatown & South

WEST LOOP

LOOP

W. Jackson Blvd.
E. Jackson Blvd.

LaSalle Van Buren

Jackson

Van Buren St.

VAN BUREN ST.

LaSalle Library

W. Van Buren

LaSalle STREET STA.

W. Congress

W. Harrison St.

Clinton St.

Canal St.

Wells St.

LaSalle St.

Clark St.

Dearborn St.

State St.

Congress Pkwy.

LaSalle Pkwy.

E. Harrison St.

Harrison

BUCKINGHAM FOUNTAIN

N

W. Polk St.

Polk St.

Chicago Curry House

W. 9th St.

Plymouth St.

E. 8th St.

Wabash Ave.

Michigan Ave.

Columbus Dr.

Balbo Dr.

GRANT PARK

HUTCHINSON ATHLETIC FIELD

AVERY FIELD

SHEDD AQUARIUM

SOUTH LOOP

E. 11th St.

Eleven City Diner

FIELD MUSEUM OF NATURAL HISTORY

Roosevelt Rd.

Roosevelt Rd.

Federal St.

E. 13th St.

Lake Shore Dr.

McFetridge Dr.

SOUTH

14th St.

COTTON TAIL PARK

SOLDIER FIELD

BRANCH

Canal St.

W. 16th St.

E. 16th St.

Waldron Dr.

Clark St.

Acadia

Prairie Ave.

W. 18th St.

18th St.

E. 18th St.

Calumet Ave.

PING TOM MEM. PARK

Wentworth Ave.

S. Tan Ct.

19th St.

Wabash Ave.

Cullerton St.

Cullerton St.

CHINATOWN

MCCB

Archer Ave.

Phoenix

E. 21st St.

MingHin

Cermak-Chinatown

Cermak-McCormick Place

Cermak Rd.

Dolo

Cermak Rd.

E. Cermak Rd.

Daguan Noodle

Grove St.

Princeton Ave.

W. 23rd St.

23rd Pl.

Federal St.

Dearborn St.

State St.

E. 23rd St.

McCORMICK PLACE

W. 24th St.

24th Pl.

E. 24th St.

Michigan Ave.

Stewart Ave.

W. 25th Pl.

PARK NO. 540

25th St.

Hyde Park

W. 26th St.

E. 26th St.

53rd St.

The Promontory

Dorchester Ave.

Blackstone Ave.

Harper Ave.

Lake Park Ave.

SPRUCE PARK

54th St.

90 94

W. 27th St.

W. 27th St.

E. 28th St.

HYDE PARK

PILSEN, UNIVERSITY VILLAGE & BRIDGEPORT

PILSEN, UNIVERSITY VILLAGE & BRIDGEPORT

its signature squares with both sweet and savory flavors. Varieties like cheddar cheese are topped with coffee-braised short ribs, while red velvet waffles come with strawberry compote and whipped cream cheese. As long as you're adding to your cholesterol count, stop at one of the many locations of **Ricobene's** for a breaded steak sandwich or a big slab of juicy barbecue ribs.

If you're strolling through the Museum Campus for lunch, grab cash for a bite at **Kim & Carlo's Hot Dog Cart** between the Field Museum and Shedd Aquarium. Vegetarians applaud their special veggie dog with all the Chicago toppings, while everyone gets a great skyline view from Grant Park. For a glimpse of real Windy City politics in action, grab a seat at **Manny's**, the venerable coffee shop and deli. Then sink your teeth into a giant pastrami on rye or a plate of crispy potato pancakes while watching the city's wheelers and dealers do business.

When night falls, the South Loop really gets rocking. Buddy Guy himself often hits the stage at **Buddy Guy's Legends**, where live blues ring out nightly. Catch a set while digging into classic Southern soul food like fried okra, gumbo, or jambalaya. Similarly, the **Velvet Lounge**, founded by late jazz legend Fred Anderson, moved from

its original location in 2006, but still puts on a heckuva show. Other cutting edge and contemporary musicians also perform here several times a week. For a blast from the past but of a different sort, comedy and history come together at **Tommy Gun's Garage**. This dolled-up speakeasy hosts a riotous dinner theater that also allows the audience to participate.

CHINATOWN

That ornate and arched gate at Wentworth Avenue and Cermak Road welcomes locals and visitors alike to one of the largest Chinatowns in America. This iconic structure is an apt symbol for the neighborhood, where the local population is still predominantly Chinese-American and history happily co-exists with contemporary life. The two-story outdoor **Chinatown Square** mall encompasses everything from restaurants and small boutiques to big banks, thereby giving the community a buzzing culinary and cultural introduction. Many of the restaurants here offer classic Chinese-American fare that is an amalgam of Sichuan and Cantonese cuisines, but for a homemade spread stock up on all things authentic from **Chinatown Market**. This large and crowded "super" store is outfitted with endless rows of Lee Kum Kee sauces, seafood, fresh produce, and more. At local standby **Go 4 Food**, a Sichuan beef lunch combo or wok-fried and hundred-spiced chicken continue to sate those pungent palates.

Let the kids pick out a few intriguing Japanese sweets at **Aji Ichiban**, housed in the Chinatown Square mall, where bins filled with rainbows of foil-wrapped Japanese candy offer opportunities for tricks or treats. Unless you can read the characters on the wrappers, you're in for a surprise—though the store offers samples before charging by the pound. Home cooks as well as haute chefs know Chinatown isn't just a destination for dining out. It's also great for filling up on all the good eats necessary for a great home-cooked meal. In fact, the entire neighborhood is a specialty marketplace of sorts: find a mind-boggling array of fresh-pulled noodles at **Mayflower Food**; while Hong Kong-based tea shop, **Saint's Alp Teahouse**, serves quick snacks and a variety of tea-based drinks including the widely popular milk tea and taro milk tea—with or without tapioca pearls. Freshly baked fortune and almond cookies are a revelation at **Golden Dragon Fortune Cookies**, but those craving a wider range of sweets may pour over the cases at **Chiu Quon Bakery** filled with cakes and other cream- or custard-filled pastries. Meanwhile, additional inspiration can be found by perusing a cookbook or two from the Chinatown branch of Chicago's Public Library. Finally, pay homage to the perennial city pastime by watching the White Sox do their thing on Guaranteed Rate Field, or the "Monsters of the Midway" take the gridiron inside Soldier Field's formidable walls.

Museums and learning centers showcase the Windy City's heritage from all angles. Apart from the stately collection of historic buildings in Grant Park's Museum Campus, this neighborhood is also home to Willie Dixon's Blues Heaven Foundation, whose mission is to preserve its musical legacy. With swooping green roof ornaments, the Harold Washington Library Center is impossible to miss, but an equally worthy site is their glass-ceilinged winter garden hidden inside.

ACADIA ✿ ✿

Contemporary · *Luxury*

🍸 ♿ 🔲 🍽️

MAP: B3

One of the true gems of South Loop, Acadia is the impassioned restaurant of the talented Ryan McCaskey. Pulling from his Vietnamese heritage as well as his travels in Maine, Chef McCaskey's cooking is ambitious, precise and deliciously technical. Perhaps even more importantly, his kitchen's commitment to that vision is palpable in every bite.

Set between glassy apartment buildings and a small patch of grass, Acadia is a distinct stand-alone destination. The interior is decidedly elegant, with soaring ceilings and a soothing blend of warm neutrals, cool grays, as well as chocolate and sage peppered throughout the lofty space. Service is gracious and professional—the kind we all hope for but rarely find these days.

A guest at the bar can choose from an à la carte menu; while the dining room offers a seven-course feast. A meal in this brigade's sure hands might reveal an Isle au Haut scallop fresh off the coast of Maine, set over a raviolo filled with pastura con trufa cheese, ramps, morels and sumptuously finished with Normande sauce. The signature Yukon gold potato "risotto" studded with tender leeks, sweet English peas, savory morels and truffle butter is pure exquisiteness.

🟦 1639 S. Wabash Ave. (bet. 16th & 18th Sts.)

🚇 Cermak-Chinatown

📞 (312) 360-9500 — **WEB:** www.acadiachicago.com

🟦 Dinner Wed – Sun   **PRICE:** $$$$

CHICAGO CURRY HOUSE 🍴

Indian · Elegant

♿ 🚪

MAP: B2

Maybe you sniff the wafting aromas of ginger, garlic, and cumin first; maybe you hear the sitar tinkling its welcoming notes as you enter. Either way, you know immediately that Chicago Curry House is a commendable showcase of Indian and Nepalese cuisines.

The lunchtime buffet lets you eat your fill with crispy papadum and baskets of naan; while dinner features an à la carte of faves including Nepalese khasi ko maasu, with bone-in goat bobbing in a velvety cardamom- and black pepper-sauce. Tandoori chicken is a smoky, moist delight; and butter chicken, creamy and rich in a tomato- and garam masala-spiced gravy, is done just right. The staff has helpful suggestions for dealing with the area's draconian parking restrictions; call ahead for tips.

■ 899 S. Plymouth Ct. (at 9th St.)
🚇 Harrison
✆ (312) 362-9999 — **WEB:** www.curryhouseonline.com
■ Lunch & dinner daily   **PRICE:** 🍜

DAGUAN NOODLE 😊

Chinese · Simple

♿

MAP: A4

Nonne have their minestrone, nanas have their chicken noodle soup, but for the best in comfort food Chinese-style, there's nothing better than these rice noodles in soup. The broth is prepared daily and whether you choose sour or spicy, or even the pig intestine and oxtail version, it tastes like liquid gold. Consuming this creation is great fun too, with a tray of vegetables and choice of protein—perhaps Chinese potted meats or flaky shrimp cake? Then, drop those bouncy rice noodles into the bubbling pot and wait for the magic to unfold. Regulars may round out this feast with such sumptuous sides as steamed pork buns, a cucumber salad or fluffy pumpkin pancakes.

The gleaming space is small but doesn't accept reservations (yet!), so expect a wait.

■ 2230 South Wentworth Ave. (bet. 23rd Pl. & 24th St.)
🚇 Cermak-Chinatown
✆ (312) 929-2758 — **WEB:** N/A
■ Lunch & dinner daily   **PRICE:** 🍜

DOLO

Chinese • Contemporary décor

MAP: A4

Settled amidst the hustle and bustle of Archer Avenue is this rare and stylish gem. Dolo is welcoming and accessible, with a highly engaged service staff, a full modern bar and plenty of on-site parking. And though it's a stone's throw from Cermak, it feels like a tucked-away treasure for locals in the know.

While there's dim sum to be had, diners would do well to try their hand at the impressive specialty menu. Jellyfish is cut into tiny slivers and laced with a heavenly blend of chili oil and Sichuan peppercorns. Following this, creamy, steamed sea bass may be paired with pickled peppers, fragrant ginger, scallion and cilantro. For dinner, the tea-flavored chicken brined for two whole days, is the very essence of tenderness.

2222 S. Archer Ave. (bet. Princeton & Steward Aves.)
Cermak-Chinatown
(312) 877-5117 — **WEB:** www.dolorestaurant.com
Lunch & dinner daily — PRICE: $$

ELEVEN CITY DINER

Deli • Family

MAP: B2

Nosh on a mile-high sandwich or chocolate malt at Eleven City Diner, a modern revival of the classic Jewish deli. Gleaming subway tiles play off retro leather booths and swiveling barstools, while jazz in the background keeps things moving with chutzpah and finesse.

Diner standards include patty melts, sandwiches piled with corned beef or pastrami, knishes and latkes. Bubbe's chicken soup comes brimming with a fluffy matzo ball the size of a baseball; while Junior's cheesecake from Brooklyn or a triple-decker wedge of red velvet cake sates all the sweet-loving guests. A full-service deli counter offers salamis and smoked fish to-go. For a true blast from the past, stop by the candy stand near the entry, stocked with Bazooka Joe and other favorites.

1112 S. Wabash Ave. (bet. 11th St. & Roosevelt Rd.)
Roosevelt
(312) 212-1112 — **WEB:** www.elevencitydiner.com
Lunch & dinner daily — PRICE:

MCCB

Chinese • Contemporary décor

MAP: A4

Modern Chinese Cookbook is the explanation behind the acronym of this modern retreat, tucked inside the sprawling Chinatown Square. You'll understand the name once you catch sight of their menu—it's a bible brimming with delicious selections leaning toward spicy Sichuan flavors.

Meat or fish cooked over applewood charcoal originated as a street food in Chongqing. But here it's one of the more unique items, and may be tailed by the equal parts spicy and sour pickle- and fish-soup, which packs a wallop for such a wee bowl. Finally, this kitchen also turns out an excellent version of wok-fried rabbit with cumin, peppercorn and cilantro, but their salt and pepper shrimp can't be skipped. Full of flavor with a brittle shell, these beauties are hard to resist.

- 2138 S. Archer Ave. (Inside Chinatown Sq.)
- Cermak-Chinatown
- (312) 881-0168 — **WEB:** www.mccbchicago.com
- Lunch & dinner daily   **PRICE:** $$

MINGHIN

Chinese • Chic

MAP: A4

Conveniently situated on the ground level of Chinatown Square, MingHin is a stylish standby that draws a diverse crowd to the neighborhood. Spacious dining rooms separated by wooden lattice panels offer seating for a number of occasions, from casual booths and large banquet-style rounds to specially outfitted tables for hot pots.

Dim sum is a popular choice even on weekdays, with diners making selections from photographic menus rather than waiting for a passing cart. Among the numerous options, juicy har gao, stuffed with plump seasoned shrimp, always hits the spot. Pan-fried turnip cakes are simultaneously crispy and creamy, studded with bits of pork and mushroom. Fluffy and subtly sweet Malay steamed egg cake is a rare find for dessert.

- 2168 S. Archer Ave. (at Princeton Ave.)
- Cermak-Chinatown
- (312) 808-1999 — **WEB:** www.minghincuisine.com
- Lunch & dinner daily   **PRICE:** $$

PHOENIX

Chinese • *Family*

MAP: A4

Dim sum lovers get the best of both worlds at Phoenix, a comfortable room that boasts a grand view of the Chicago skyline. Here, stacks of bamboo baskets are wheeled to tables on signature silver trolleys for a classic experience—yet each diner's selection is cooked to order for fresh and steaming-hot bites. The proof is in the soft and poppable shrimp-and-chive dumplings and the fluffy white buns stuffed with chunks of barbecue pork.

Those looking for larger portions will appreciate the meandering menu, which also boasts Hong Kong-style stir-fry and clay pot dishes alongside Americanized Chinese classics. Fillets of steamed sea bass swim in soy oil on a large oval platter, sprinkled with a touch of slivered scallion to brighten the delicately flaky fish.

- 2131 S. Archer Ave. (bet. Princeton & Wentworth Aves.)
- Cermak-Chinatown
- (312) 328-0848 — **WEB:** www.chinatownphoenix.com
- Lunch & dinner daily   **PRICE:** 🥢

THE PROMONTORY

American • *Trendy*

MAP: C5

The Promontory has brought a bright and bustling gathering place to the Hyde Park community and you'll easily lose track of time while listening to the DJ-curated groovy tunes. Under lofty ceilings trimmed with black iron beams and sleek wood accents, urbanites sip hand-crafted cocktails around a central bar.

A white-hot fire blazes away in the open kitchen, providing the "hearth to table" food trumpeted on the menu. Banish bad memories of soggy lunchboxes and go for the fried bologna sandwich, with thick slices of house-cured bologna crisped on the griddle, then paired with tart sauerkraut, melted Swiss cheese and folded into marble rye. Banana-nut bread with whipped cream, caramelized banana slices and loads of syrup makes for a nice dessert.

- 5311 S. Lake Park Ave. West (bet. 53rd & 54th Sts.)
- (312) 801-2100 — **WEB:** www.promontorychicago.com
- Lunch & dinner daily   **PRICE:** $$

GOLD COAST

GLITZ & GLAMOUR

The moniker says it all: the Gold Coast is one of the Windy City's poshest neighborhoods, flaunting everything from swanky high-rises along Lake Shore Drive to dazzling boutiques dotting Michigan Avenue. Stroll down the Magnificent Mile only to discover that money can indeed buy it all. Then, head over to Oak Street for yet another spree and watch millionaires mingle over martinis while heiresses rummage for handbags.

APPLAUDING THE ARTS

Through all this allure, Gold Coast architecture is not just notable but stunning. And, mansions crafted in regal Queen Anne, Georgian Revival, or Richardsonian Romanesque styles are unequivocally breathtaking. However, this neighborhood is not all about the glitz; it is also deeply committed to the arts as a whole, housing both the Museum of Contemporary Art and the world-leading Newberry Library. Culture vultures are sure to uncover something edgy and unique at A Red Orchid Theater, after which the exotic Indian lunchtime buffet at **Gaylord** seems not only opportune, but perhaps obligatory? This prized subterranean location, with its spelled-out menu items and well-stocked bar, is sought by both aficionados as well as anyone hungering for free appetizers during happy hour. Nearby, **Le Cordon Bleu College of Culinary Arts** continues to train students (read: hot chefs in the making) on the classics, as well as the next food fad in Chicago's kitchens.

RAUCOUS NIGHTS

It's a well-known fact that the Gold Coast also knows how to party. Visit any nightclub, pub, or restaurant along Rush and Division to get a sense of how the cool kids hold it down—until well after dawn. By then,

find breakfast on the burner at **The Original Pancake House**. This may seem like a lowbrow treat for such a high-brow neighborhood, but really can there be anything more rewarding than fluffy pancakes, towering waffles, and sizzling skillet eggs after a late night?

There is also some darn good junk food to be had in this white-gloved capital of chic. American comfort classics like sliders, burgers, and mac and cheese find their way into the menu at **LuxBar**, a dynamic lounge-cum-bar that proffers some of the best people-watching in town. Need some sweet? Make your way to one of **Teuscher's** outposts for decadent dark chocolate or even **Corner Bakery Cafe** for a fleet of bakery fresh treats—the golden-brown cinnamon crème cake topped with crumbles of cinnamon streusel and powdered sugar has been drawing residents for over two decades now and is (rightfully) dubbed a signature.

A QUICK FIX

With so many awards under its belt and boasting the best ingredients in town, **Gold Coast Dogs** is packed to the gills (er, buns), perpetually. Inside, everyone is either a regular or on the verge of

becoming one—thanks in large part to their deliciously charred dogs, usually topped with gooey cheddar. Or, simply humor your hot dog hankering by joining the constant queue outside **Downtown Dogs**. Surely these robust eats should be sealed by a cup that revives? **TeaGschwendner** is just the spot where locals have been known to lose themselves in a world of exotic selections. And, if you don't feel like steeping your own "Sencha Claus" blend, then snag a seat at **Argo Tea** where clouds of whipped cream and flavorful iced drinks are all part of the carte—it's just like Starbucks without the coffee!

HEAVEN ON EARTH

In keeping with its quintessentially elegant and old-world reputation, the Gold Coast also allows you to don your Grandmother's pearls for afternoon tea at **The Drake's Palm Court**. Daintily sip, never slurp, your tea while listening to the gentle strumming of a harp and sampling a divine selection of their finger sandwiches, flaky pastries, and buttery scones. If it's good enough for the Queen, it will certainly do. Also housed in The Drake is warm and luxurious **Coq d'Or**, famous for its spectrum of classic cocktails, comfort food specials, and live weekend entertainment. And finally, over on Delaware Place, fine wines along with cocktails aren't the only thing heating up the scene at **Drumbar**—a rooftop scene at the Raffaello Hotel that lets the fashionable crowd frolic alfresco at all hours of the night.

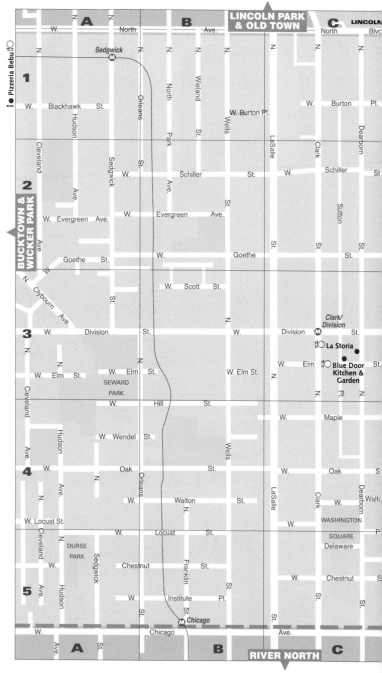

A   B   C

W.   North   Ave.

North   Blvd

O Pizzeria Bebu

Sedgwick Ⓜ

N.

N.

N.

N.

N.

N.

1

W. Blackhawk   St.

Hudson

Orleans

North

Wieland

Wells

W. Burton Pl.

W.   Burton   Pl.

Cleveland

St.

Sedgwick

Park

Ave.

W.   Schiller

St.

LaSalle

Clark

W.   Schiller   St

2

Ave.

W. Evergreen   Ave.

W.   Evergreen   Ave.

St.

Sutton

St.

St.

Ave.

Goethe   St.

St.

W.

Goethe

St.

St.

St.

N. Clybourn Ave.

W.   Scott   St.

N.

Clark/
Division Ⓜ

3

W.   Division   St.

W.

Division Ⓜ   St.

🍴O La Storia

W.   Elm   St.

N.

W.   Elm   St.

W. Elm St.

W.   Elm

🍴O **Blue Door**
Kitchen &
Garden

St.

Cleveland

SEWARD
PARK

Hill   St.

N.

Pl.

N.

W.   Maple

W.   Wendel   St.

W.

Hudson

Ave.

N.

Oak

Orleans

St.

Wells

W.   Oak   S

4

W.

N.

W.   Walton   St.

LaSalle

Clark

Dearborn

W.   Walto

W. Locust St.

N.

WASHINGTON

W.

Cleveland

W.   Locust   St.

SQUARE

P

DURSE
PARK

Delaware

Sedgwick

W.   Chestnut   St.

Franklin

St.

W.   Chestnut   St

5

Ave.

Hudson

St.

W.   Institute   Pl.

St.

St.

St.

St.   *Chicago* Ⓜ

W.   Chicago   Ave.

A   B   C

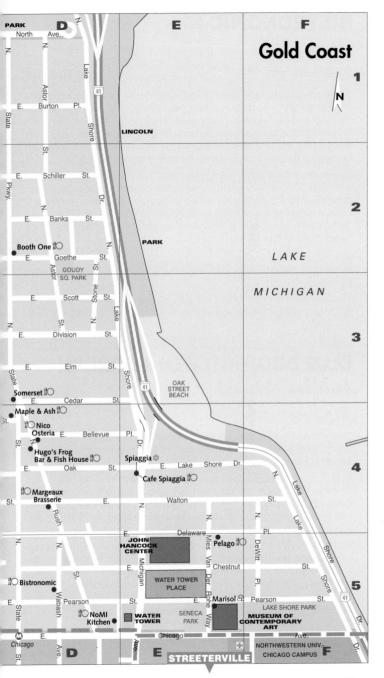

PARK
North Ave.
D
E
F

Gold Coast

1

N

Astor
E. Burton Pl.
State
Lake Shore Dr.

LINCOLN

St.
E. Schiller St.
Pkwy.
N.
E. Banks St.

2

● Booth One ‖○
E. Goethe St.
GOUDY SQ. PARK
Astor St.
E. Scott St.
N. St.
E. Division St.

LAKE

MICHIGAN

PARK

3

E. Elm St.

E. Cedar St.

OAK STREET BEACH

● Somerset ‖○
State

● Maple & Ash ‖○
St.
‖○ Nico Osteria
E. Bellevue Pl.
St.
● Hugo's Frog Bar & Fish House ‖○
Spiaggia ❄
Dr.

E. Oak St.
● Cafe Spiaggia ‖○
E. Lake Shore Dr.

4

‖○ Margeaux Brasserie
St.
E. Walton St.
Rush St.
N.
N.
Lake Shore Dr.

E. Delaware Pl.
● Pelago ‖○
N.
Mies Van Der Rohe Way
DeWitt

JOHN HANCOCK CENTER

‖○ Bistronomic
St.
E. Chestnut St.
St.
Michigan
Lake Shore Dr.

Wabash
E. Pearson St.
WATER TOWER PLACE
Marisol ⚕
E. Pearson St.
LAKE SHORE PARK

5

‖○ NoMI Kitchen
WATER TOWER
SENECA PARK
MUSEUM OF CONTEMPORARY ART

Ⓜ Chicago
E. Chicago Ave.
NORTHWESTERN UNIV. CHICAGO CAMPUS
St.
D
E
F
Dr.

STREETERVILLE

69

CHICAGO ▲ GOLD COAST

BISTRONOMIC
French • Bistro

MAP: D5

Tucked away from the buzz of the Magnificent Mile, Bistronomic is a great place to cool your tired heels. Jaunty red awnings beckon brightly, and the revolving door spins guests into a warm room that's focused on the bonhomie of dining with friends. Oxblood walls, gray banquettes and a central bar play up the bistro feel, while the kitchen conveys creativity with fresh renditions of tasty classics.

Rusticity and elegance come together in a fillet of Lake Superior whitefish that is pan-seared to golden-brown and matched with spring ratatouille, preserved lemon and puréed eggplant. Exquisitely crisp feuilletine is a glamorous upgrade to the classic Kit Kat bar, folded with hazelnuts, bittersweet chocolate and finished with a sweet-tart orange sauce.

■ 840 N. Wabash Ave. (bet. Chestnut & Pearson Sts.)
▣ Chicago (Red)
✆ (312) 944-8400 — **WEB:** www.bistronomic.net
■ Lunch Wed – Sun Dinner nightly   **PRICE: $$**

BLUE DOOR KITCHEN & GARDEN
American • Elegant

MAP: C3

Thank chef-to-the-stars Art Smith for raising the stakes of the local dining scene with this relaxed bistro, which replaces his former success, Table 52.

In 1871, this carriage house home is said to have survived the Great Chicago Fire. Today, the cozy and well-appointed dining room makes the most of its parquet floors, Louis XV-style chairs, welcoming bar and open kitchen where Southern-leaning fare is prepared in full view.

The cooking showcases produce from The Farm, located just an hour south of the city, so seasonal dishes like tomato and watermelon salad over greens will be particularly refreshing. Signature desserts, like the towering slice of Hummingbird cake layered with banana and pineapple, are enough to feed two (if not four) diners.

■ 52 W. Elm St. (bet. Clark & Dearborn Sts.)
▣ Clark/Division
✆ (312) 573-4000 — **WEB:** www.bluedoorkitchenchicago.com
■ Lunch & dinner daily   **PRICE: $$**

BOOTH ONE

International • Contemporary décor

MAP: D2

Booth One's opening marks the return of one of Chicago's trendiest dining rooms. Formerly known as The Pump Room, this contemporary reincarnation is named after the booth reserved for A-list celebs who dined there—have a look at the black-and-white photos lining the walls for a glimpse of the good old days. Today, the stylish interior flaunts a plush cream, gold and gray color scheme.

The food is an old-timey homage to European cooking and is as ambitious as it is excellent. Classic dishes include beef Wellington, Dover sole and rack of lamb. Alternatively, make a meal of American faves like lobster Louie salad or a burger. Desserts are especially nice, including a slice of devil's food cake layered with coconut mousse and topped with warm fudge sauce.

- 1301 N. State Pkwy. (at Goethe St.)
- Clark/Division
- (312) 649-0535 — **WEB:** www.boothone.com
- Lunch & dinner daily

PRICE: $$$

CAFE SPIAGGIA

Italian • Chic

MAP: E4

Welcome to the less formal, more approachable, all-day extension of Tony Mantuano's grande-dame Spiaggia, located just next door. The setting of this café is relaxed yet stylish; and dining here is a great way to enjoy unforgettable lakeside views for a fraction of the cost as its namesake.

Expect a casual menu of simple lunchtime bites and sandwiches that gives way to a more composed yet still appetizing offering at dinner. But regardless of when you visit, house-made pastas are sure to be a particular highlight, especially those short tubes of lumache bathed with a rich and rustic lamb ragù. Don't miss out on generous portions of their fun and creative desserts, like pizzelle cookies sandwiching toasted milk gelato with chocolate-hazelnut crunch.

- 980 N. Michigan Ave. (at Oak St.)
- Chicago (Red)
- (312) 280-2750 — **WEB:** www.spiaggiarestaurant.com/cafe
- Lunch Mon – Sat Dinner nightly

PRICE: $$

HUGO'S FROG BAR & FISH HOUSE 🍴

American • *Fashionable*

MAP: D4

Housed in a sprawling setting adjacent to big brother Gibson's, Hugo's always seems packed. The vast dining room sets white linen-topped tables amid dark polished wood and pale walls decorated with a mounted swordfish, fish prints and model ships. Hugo's bar draws its own crowd with abundant counter seating.

The menu focuses on a selection of fish preparations as well as steaks and chops. These are supplemented by stone crab claws, oysters, crab cakes, chowders and sautéed frog's legs. Speaking of which, the restaurant takes its name from the nickname of owner Hugo Ralli's grandfather, General Bruce Hay of Her Majesty's Imperial Forces.

Bring a football team to share a slice of the Muddy Bottom Pie, a decadent (and enormous) ice cream cake.

◾ 1024 N. Rush St. (bet. Bellevue Pl. & Oak St.)
🚇 Clark/Division
✆ (312) 640-0999 — **WEB:** www.hugosfrogbar.com
◾ Lunch Sat – Sun Dinner nightly   **PRICE: $$**

LA STORIA 🍴

Italian • *Elegant*

MAP: C3

Tucked into a gorgeous townhouse along Chicago's Gold Coast, this Italian charmer woos with pretty patios, sexy dark panel walls and conversation-worthy murals by Edward Sorel. The result is a casual, clubby feel; and the first floor, with its low wood beam ceilings, offers great views of Dearborn Street.

Chef Rey Villalobos, who oversees the rest of Ideology's portfolio of restaurants (including Blue Door Farm Stand and Chicago Q), takes the reins here, pushing out a finely executed Italian menu. Try the notable pollo Milanese. While it may seems like a predictable standard, La Storia's version is laid over excellent liver mousse and strewn with crispy fried capers as well as peppery watercress to give it a solid leg up on the competition.

◾ 1154 N. Dearborn St. (bet. Division & Elm Sts.)
🚇 Clark/Division
✆ (312) 915-5950 — **WEB:** www.lastoriachicago.com
◾ Dinner Tue – Sun   **PRICE: $$$**

MAPLE & ASH

Steakhouse • Fashionable

MAP: D4

Did someone say scene? Oh darling, that's half the fun at Chicago's buzziest steakhouse, Maple & Ash. Deep-set leather couches, clubby music and even a photo booth lend the multi-level marvel an irresistible party vibe.

This restaurant is set to the soft glow emanating from the semi-open kitchen, where a wood-fired hearth lights up dry-aged steakhouse classics, cut to generous proportions. Seafood lovers will find plenty to mull over too, like a tangle of octopus and squid, prepared in the wood-fueled oven and served with dill yogurt, arugula and roasted potatoes. Then, a fire-roasted seafood tower is brought tableside, featuring lobster tail, scallops, Manilla clams and king crab, all bathed in garlic butter, chili oil and served with house-made pasta.

 8 W. Maple St. (bet. Dearborn & State Sts.)

 Clark/Division

 (312) 944-8888 — **WEB:** www.mapleandash.com

 Lunch Sun Dinner nightly   **PRICE: $$$$**

MARGEAUX BRASSERIE

French • Elegant

MAP: D4

Margeaux Brasserie is one swank spot. Housed inside the Waldorf Astoria, this restaurant marks the first Chicago venture for the popular Mina Group, led by esteemed San Francisco-based chef, Michael Mina. The space is bright and airy, with light streaming in through the large picture windows and lots of luxe velvet and leather details.

Kick things off with perfectly caramelized duck wings a' l'orange. Diners may then choose to linger over dishes like the warm tomato Tatin, paired with puff pastry, Camembert and pistou. While a bone-in rack of lamb takes satisfaction to the next level when coupled with stewed chickpeas, piquillos and fennel, turnip with roasted lamb jus and a croustillant filled with braised lamb rib is the very picture of decadence.

 11 E. Walton St. (at Rush St.)

 Chicago (Red)

 (312) 625-1324 — **WEB:** www.michaelmina.net

 Lunch Sat – Sun Dinner nightly   **PRICE: $$$**

MARISOL

American • Contemporary décor

MAP: E5

Despite its location on the first floor of the Museum of Contemporary Art, Marisol is so much more than a museum food court. This restaurant takes its name from the late French pop art sculptor, whose work was the museum's first acquisition.

The local, seasonal and sensible cooking appeals to all palates, though much of the menu focuses on vegetables. Start with a duo of raw and char-grilled rapini, tossed with pepitas, bits of flavorful n'duja and set over a smear of garlicky aïoli to experience a plate that wins on every level. This kitchen also knows how to roast a soul-warming chicken, served with new potatoes and green garlic-pan sauce. If your appetite permits, savor the miso-butterscotch pudding finished with satsuma, macadamias and puffed rice.

- 205 E. Pearson St. (at Mies Van Der Rohe Way)
- Chicago (Red)
- (312) 799-3599 — **WEB:** www.marisolchicago.com
- Lunch Tue – Sun Dinner Tue – Sat   PRICE: $$

NICO OSTERIA

Italian • Contemporary décor

MAP: D4

Buzzworthy and a hit since day one, Chef Paul Kahan's local darling happens to be one of the most likeable restaurants in town. Think of it as more trendsetting than trendy. The dining room has a stylish look, with Mediterranean tile floors and plenty of natural light. The accommodating staff ensures that no one leaves disappointed.

The carte focuses on Italian-leaning seafood dishes, so it is an ideal stop for inspired crudo like fluke with ice-wine vinegar, fennel and breadcrumbs. Take a counter seat before the open kitchen to see just how the Kindai tuna with black trumpet mushrooms and kumquat comes together. The regional menu may also go on to highlight such boldly flavored oceanic treats as chili-cured swordfish with thin, house-made grissini.

- 1015 N. Rush St. (at Bellevue Pl.)
- Chicago (Brown)
- (312) 994-7100 — **WEB:** www.nicoosteria.com
- Lunch & dinner daily   PRICE: $$$

NOMI KITCHEN 🍴

American • *Contemporary décor*

MAP: D5

A hushed aerie awaits on the seventh floor of the Park Hyatt at NoMI Kitchen. Let the dapper staff whisk you through the hotel lobby and elevator to a glassed-in dining room with Water Tower views. A semi-open kitchen doesn't detract from the lush but restrained décor, and a breezy terrace offers an alfresco option with a different menu.

The kitchen's impressive and ingredient-driven dishes showcase seasonal American cuisine. Roasted carrots with goat cheese and popped quinoa are a nice opener before moving on to the rustic and flavorful house made pork sausage over a bed of roasted Yukon potatoes, charred onions and whole garlic. End on a sweet-tart note with the key lime curd in a black pepper tart shell.

- 800 N. Michigan Ave. (entrance on Chicago Ave.)
- Chicago (Red)
- (312) 239-4030 — **WEB:** www.nomirestaurant.com
- Lunch & dinner daily   PRICE: $$$

PELAGO 🍴

Italian • *Elegant*

MAP: E5

This jewel box of a spot is fittingly set adjacent to the Raffaello Hotel. Oozing with elegance, it boasts a crisp style via large windows, tasteful artwork and comfortable leather seats. An azure-blue color theme ensures the mood is serene. If the décor doesn't evoke the Med, then the Italian-leaning dishes will do the trick. Baked lasagna layered with tender noodles, tomato sauce, béchamel and veal ragù is both delicate and satisfying. A rustic, pan-roasted pork chop cooked a-la-Nonna-style and sided by mashed potatoes is particularly comforting.

Some may swap dessert for cheese, but the spumoni, a frozen vanilla sabayon sliced into triangular wedges and topped with fresh strawberries, is a light, slightly-sweet, and elegant finish.

- 201 E. Delaware Pl. (at Mies van der Rohe Way)
- Chicago (Red)
- (312) 280-0700 — **WEB:** www.pelagorestaurant.com
- Lunch & dinner daily   PRICE: $$$

PIZZERIA BEBU

Pizza • Contemporary décor

MAP: N/A

Chicago and pizza go together like peanut butter and jelly, but does the Windy City need yet another shop dedicated to the crusty stuff? If it is Pizzeria Bebu, you bet your brick-lined gas (oven) it does. This excellent rendition gives any of its kind a run for their money.

A crispy crust with cornicione that crackles with flavor—this is a first-class pizza. You can't go wrong here, whether you veer simple with a Margherita (San Marzano tomatoes and mozzarella); have a little fun (crumbled meatballs, giardiniera, ricotta cheese and parmesan); or go nutty with nutless pesto, vodka sauce and fresh mozzarella. Pizzas may be the star at this gleaming, modern restaurant, but the thick and fluffy frittata proves that their other staples deserve equal billing.

■ 1521 N. Fremont St. (bet. Weed & Blackhawk Sts.)
■ North/Clybourn
✆ (312) 280-6000 — **WEB:** www.bebu.pizza
■ Lunch & dinner daily

PRICE: $$

SOMERSET

American • Design

MAP: D3

If the Great Gatsby himself opened a restaurant, it might look something like the unabashedly gorgeous Somerset, the Boka Restaurant Group's long-awaited sashay into the Gold Coast dining scene. And what an arrival indeed—nestled within the stylish Viceroy hotel and featuring what can only be described as a sublime yacht-club décor, with gilded mirrors, curvy blue banquettes and luminous art deco light fixtures.

Chef Lee Wolen's seasonal American cuisine is beautifully executed and surprising in all the right ways. Don't miss the smoked beet tartare, elevated to such heights you might never go back to beef, or flawless squid ink chitarra. A deconstructed carrot cake, tucked with buckwheat tuille, cream cheese mousse and blood orange, is divine.

■ 1112 N. State St. (bet Franklin & Wells Sts.)
■ Clark/Division
✆ (312) 586-2150 — **WEB:** www.somersetchicago.com
■ Lunch & dinner daily

PRICE: $$$

SPIAGGIA

Italian • Elegant

MAP: E4

There are many reasons why Spiaggia remains one of Chicago's most beloved Italian restaurants. There are high-end bells and whistles aplenty, but to hear the staff recite the effort and intricacies behind, say, the culurgiones is to compel you to order them.

History isn't just on offer, it's celebrated here, where the bucatini pulls from the archives to show off a recipe from 1985. Bread is a noteworthy artisanal assortment, including a crusty sesame seed-coated morsel begging to be smeared with whipped ricotta. Tutto il coniglio, a gorgeous presentation of sliced rabbit loin stuffed with forcemeat, is buoyed by flavorful lentils cooked in rabbit stock and a bowl of decadent blue corn polenta with shredded braised rabbit meat that is just oh-so-good. Up for something sweet? Olive oil cake layered with white chocolate mousse, topped with yuzu gelee, and composed with torched honey meringue as well as honey ice cream is a superb choice.

All in all, to dine at Spiaggia is to celebrate a Chicago grande-dame. The stunning dining room is designed with marble columns and alcoves to enhance the most of its dramatic views and makes for an idyllic spot to appreciate the Magnificent Mile by night.

▨ 980 N. Michigan Ave. (at Oak St.)

▨ Chicago (Red)

✆ (312) 280-2750 — **WEB:** www.spiaggiarestaurant.com

▨ Dinner nightly **PRICE: $$$$**

A charming pair of lively North Side neighborhoods, Humboldt Park and Logan Square have long been revered as Chicagoland's heart and soul. They may reside a few steps off the beaten path, but these locals still live to eat and can be found perusing the wares of global grocers, secret bodegas, and those fine falafel shops. **Smalls** is one such tasty smoke hut that churns out familiar barbecue dishes alongside Asian comfort food.

Here, hickory-smoked brisket on Texas toast with Thai-style "tiger cry" sauce has earned an army of devotees for good reason. Koreatown is a prized thoroughfare spanning miles along Lawrence Avenue and preparing faithful meals that commence with banchan, followed by galbi, bulgogi, or bibimbap. **Joong Boo Market** is a gem in Avondale flaunting specialties from rice cakes and ground red pepper flakes to dried vegetables and seaweed

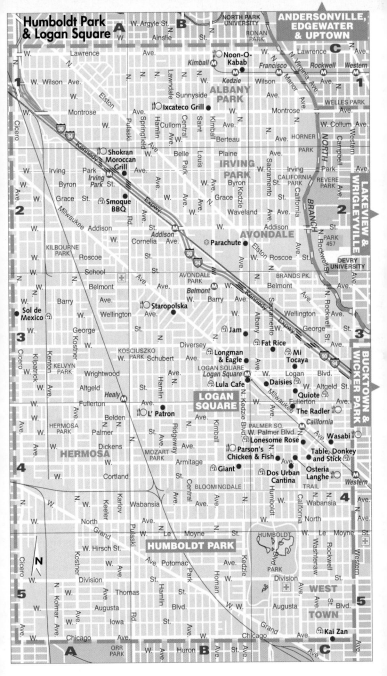

Humboldt Park & Logan Square

A   **B**   **C**

W. Argyle St.

W. Ainslie St.

NORTH PARK UNIVERSITY

RONAN PARK

ANDERSONVILLE, EDGEWATER & UPTOWN

W. Lawrence Ave.

W. Lawrence Ave.

1

Kimball

Noon-O-Kabab

N. Virginia Ave.

N. Manor Ave.

Francisco

Rockwell

Western

N. NORTH BRANCH

1

W. Wilson Ave.

Lawndale

Kedzie

Wilson

ALBANY PARK

Elston

W. Sunnyside Ave.

W. Montrose Ave.

Montrose Ave.

WELLES PARK

W. Collum Ave.

Pulaski

Ixcateco Grill

Springfield

Hamlin

Central

Saint Louis

Kimball

Kedzie

W. Cullom Ave.

W. Berteau Ave.

HORNER PARK

Campbell

Western

Kennedy Expwy.

I-90

Belle Plaine

Louis

Plaine

IRVING PARK

Irving Park

California

REVERE PARK

W. Irving Park St.

Shokran Moroccan Grill

Irving Park Rd.

W. Byron

W. Grace St.

Byron

Grace St.

Sacramento

St.

CALIFORNIA PARK

2

W. Irving Park

Milwaukee

Addison

Smoque BBQ

W. Addison St.

Waveland

Kedzie

Addison

St.

AVONDALE

Elston

Rockwell

PARK 457

2

Cornelia Ave.

Parachute

Roscoe

St.

DEVRY UNIVERSITY

KILBOURNE PARK

W. Roscoe

W. School

AVONDALE PARK

I-90

BRANDS PK.

W. Belmont Ave.

Belmont

Belmont

Sol de Mexico

W. Barry

Ave.

Staropolska

Belmont

W. Barry

Albany

Sacramento

Wellington

George

St.

Rockwell

I-90 I-94

BUCKTOWN & WICKER PARK

3

W. Wellington Ave.

KELVYN PARK

W. George St.

KOSCIUSZKO PARK

Diversey

Jam

Fat Rice

Mi Tocaya

Kenton

Klipatrick

Cicero

W. Schubert Ave.

Longman & Eagle

LOGAN SQUARE

Logan Square

Daisies

Logan Blvd.

3

W. Wrightwood Ave.

Hamlin

Lula Cafe

Kedzie Blvd.

Quiote

W. Altgeld St.

W. Altgeld

Healy

LOGAN SQUARE

Milwaukee

The Radler

California

4

W. Fullerton Ave.

L' Patron

W. Fullerton Ave.

Lonesome Rose

Palmer

Wasabi

HERMOSA PARK

W. Belden Ave.

Ridgeway

Kimball

PALMER SQ.

W. Palmer Blvd.

Dickens

MOZART PARK

W. Armitage Ave.

Parson's Chicken & Fish

Table, Donkey and Stick

Fullerton

W. Cortland St.

Giant

BLOOMINGDALE TRAIL

Dos Urban Cantina

Osteria Langhe

Western

4

HERMOSA

Keeler

Karlov

W. Wabansia Ave.

Central

Humboldt

California

Wabansia

Rockwell

Washtenaw

Western

N

W. North Ave.

Grand

W. Le Moyne St.

W. North Ave.

Le Moyne

St.

W. Hirsch St.

HUMBOLDT PARK

HUMBOLDT BLVD. PARK

W. Le Moyne St.

W. Potomac Ave.

Kedzie

Homan

Division

WEST

5

Cicero

W. Division St.

5

W. Thomas St.

Hamlin

Augusta

Blvd.

Augusta

TOWN

W. Augusta Blvd.

W. Iowa St.

Kolmar Ave.

Kostner

Pulaski Rd.

Homan

Kedzie

Grand

W. Chicago Ave.

Chicago

Ave.

Kai Zan

Western

W. Huron St.

ORR PARK

A   **B**   **C**

snacks. Stroll further along these tree-lined streets, dotted with quaint buildings and trendy shops, until you land upon **Bang Bang Pie Shop**. These handmade buttery biscuits are likely to keep you inside—indefinitely. But, make sure to step out and into **Global Garden**, a community venture (or "refugee training farm") where immigrants grow produce for sale at local farmers' markets or CSAs. Other like-minded operations include **Campbell Co-op** or **Drake Garden** whose harvest of vegetables and plants unite the neighborhood's diverse groups, while ensuring gorgeous greenery amid the city. Humboldt Park is also home to a vibrant Puerto

Rican community—just look for Paseo Boricua, the flag-shaped steel gateway demarcating the district along Division Street. Its storefronts are as much a celebration of the diaspora as the homeland, with an impressive array of traditional foods, rare ingredients, and authentic pernil. In fact, the annual **Puerto Rican Festival** features four days of festivities, fun, and great food. You can also get your fill of Caribbean cuisine in these parts, but for serious Latin food, dash over to **Café Colao**, a Puerto Rican coffee shop also selling pastries and sandwiches. Get here before the crowds for a cheese-and-guava pastellito or Cuban sandwich with cafe con leche, of course.

Bill Dugan's **The Fishguy Market** has been serving Michelin-starred restaurants for decades, while also renting space to **Wellfleet**, a popular luncheonette named after the Cape Cod fishing town. Here fish fans are always in good hands thanks to the kitchen's creative renditions of fresh crustaceans. If steaming hot

dogs are a custom in Chicago, then **Jimmy's Red Hots** is the standard bearer of this neighborhood. Meanwhile, the great value found at **Dante's Pizzeria** may only be exceeded by its larger-than-life, exceedingly tasty pies. Speaking of which, the aptly named "inferno" comes with pepperoni, sausage, bacon, and fresh garlic—just in case those blazing hot peppers aren't enough. Alternatively, take a real gamble and go for the slice of the day. Pastries take the cake at **Shokolad** and the staff at this Ukrainian haunt knows how to keep your eyes on the prize: a stacked-to-the-top glass bakery case showcases its

goodies to great effect. Their signature cheesecake lollipops may not hail from the Old Country, but rest assured that they are very tasty.

LOGAN SQUARE

An eclectic mix of cuisines combined with historic buildings and charming boulevards attracts everybody, from hipsters and working-class locals, as well as artists and students to this lovely quarter. Within the culinary community, a blend of home chefs, star cooks, and staunch foodies can be found plunging into the products at **Kurowski's Sausage Shop**, a respected butcher specializing in handmade cuts of Polish meats. Novices take note: pair a flavorful sausage with toasted rye before picking up pickles to-go from the old-school and always-reliable **Dill Pickle Food Co-op**. Then tuck into neighborhood cafe **Cellar Door Provisions** for a variety of baked-from-scratch breads, as well as European-style pastries. Carrying on this cultural explosion, Logan Square is also home to **Johnny's Grill**, a neighborhood diner that has been revived by a formally trained pastry chef. But the greasy spoon spirit lives on in dishes like the fried fish sandwich, flat top double cheeseburger, and bottomless fresh-brewed **Intelligentsia** coffee. Also of epicurean note is **Logan Square Farmers Market** selling everything ingestible from raw honey to organic zucchini; while the uniquely sourced and beautifully packaged brews at **Gaslight Coffee Roasters** are a caffeine junkie's real-life fantasy. Just as kids delight in a day spent at **Margie's Candies**, which is scattered

with homemade chocolates, adults eagerly await a night out at **Scofflaw** for gin-infused libations and secret menu combinations. Of course, the tiki craze is thriving at local cocktail legend Paul McGee's **Lost Lake Tiki Bar**, slinging rum-based delights. Food wonks however shop till they drop at **Independence Park Farmers Market** for a divine dinner back home. Less locally traditional but just as tantalizing is **Jimmy's Pizza Café**, rightfully mobbed for its mean rendition of a New York-style slice.

Albany Park is yet another melting pot of global foods and gastronomic retreats sans the sky-high prices. Plan your own Middle Eastern feast with a spectrum of cheeses, spreads, and flatbreads from **Al-Khyam Bakery & Grocery**, tailed by perfect baklava from **Nazareth Sweets**. But if meat is what you're craving, then join the crowd of carnivores at **Charcoal Delights**, a time-tested burger joint.

DAISIES 🐸

Italian • Neighborhood

MAP: C3

Kids, friends, neighbors—everyone seems to adore Daisies, and what's not to love? With its tiny, hardworking kitchen, clean, mid-century modern design and decidedly affordable prices, this local charmer can do no wrong.

Pastas reign supreme in this house, and there's even a smattering of gluten-free options. Other fun, delicious specialty dishes like the house onion dip or fried mushrooms with cheese curds show off the kitchen's playful side, along with more thoughtful creations like tajarin with chicken crackling, or mezzaluna stuffed with fermented squash and lamb. Veggie treats like braised leeks offer such intense flavor, you won't miss the meat. Finally, a thoughtful wine list celebrates domestic regions, including some from home state, Illinois.

■ 2523 N. Milwaukee (bet. Logan Blvd. & Sacramento Ave.)

🚇 Logan Square

📞 (773) 661-1671 — **WEB:** www.daisieschicago.com

■ Lunch Sun Dinner Wed – Sun

PRICE: $$

DOS URBAN CANTINA 🐸

Mexican • Contemporary décor

MAP: C4

After several years at Topolobampo, the husband-wife duo behind this gem have taken their knowledge and skills to craft this consistently delicious and inventive cuisine. And, the chefs' deep understanding of Mexican ingredients has allowed them to create elegant and well-priced compositions. Chunks of slowly braised pork carnitas are hearty, tender and brought to an entirely new level with squash that pops with bright flavor—all balanced with a bracing tomatillo broth. For dessert, indulge in an excellent Mexican sugar pie topped with whipped cream and pecan toffee that is out of this world.

The space is comfortable and roomy, so that the steady stream of thirty-somethings never make it feel crowded. Curved booths and romantic lighting lend a warm vibe.

■ 2829 W. Armitage Ave. (at Mozart St.)

📞 (773) 661-6452 — **WEB:** www.dosurbancantina.com

■ Dinner Wed – Sun

PRICE: $$

FAT RICE 👻
Macanese • *Trendy*

♿ 🛋

Not familiar with the food of Macau? Not to worry—Fat Rice turns the uninitiated into believers nightly. In fact, the restaurant's thriving success led to an expansion that includes a cocktail lounge and bakery next door. Bar seating around the open kitchen gives a bird's-eye view of the mélange of ingredients used in each dish, though servers are happy to walk any guest through the intoxicating mashup of Portuguese-meets-Asian cuisine.

Sharing is recommended for the namesake arroz gordo, a paella-esque blend of meat, shellfish and pickles. Pillowy bread pairs well with crisp chili prawns stuffed with a flavorful blend of fermented black beans and garlic; while chrysanthemum gelée served with jackfruit and peanuts is a sweet and salty thrill.

- 2957 W. Diversey Ave. (at Sacramento Ave.)
- Logan Square
- (773) 661-9170 — **WEB:** www.eatfatrice.com
- Lunch Wed – Sun Dinner Tue – Sat

PRICE: $$

GIANT 👻
American • *Trendy*

Brought to you by Jason Vincent, this fabulous and friendly restaurant is the epitome of the Windy City. Its menu is a listing of familiar dishes (think onion rings, crab salad and baby back ribs), albeit drummed up with unique accents reflecting the chef's distinctive style. The petite space is simple and lovely, with a modern-rustic décor and genuinely cozy neighborhood vibe. A chef's counter in the back offers an up-close-and-personal kitchen experience.

Kick things off with the excellent Jonah crab salad, served with soft waffle-cut potato fritters and freshly made cocktail sauce. Then move on to the "pici with chew," where thick strands of noodles are cooked to a conservative al dente, and tossed with smoky bacon, chopped jalapeños and breadcrumbs.

- 3209 W. Armitage Ave. (bet. Kedzie & Sawyer Aves.)
- (773) 252-0997 — **WEB:** www.giantrestaurant.com
- Dinner Tue – Sat

PRICE: $$

CHICAGO ▶ HUMBOLDT PARK & LOGAN SQUARE

IXCATECO GRILL

Mexican • Colorful

♿ BYO ▣

MAP: B1

Servers stand erect as soldiers at Ixcateco Grill, their pressed white shirts tucked into immaculate black pants. It's a sight you wish you'd see more often—the unmistakable feeling that the staff cares deeply about your experience at this delicious Mexican hot spot. The colorful space, painted in bright shades of orange, green and fuchsia, only adds to the bonhomie.

Chef Anselmo Ramírez, a veteran of Frontera Grill and Topolobampo, knows his way around Southern Mexican food. Try the irresistible picaditas, a pair of tender little masa canoes filled with savory chicken carnitas, pickled cactus, avocado cream and queso fresco; or the wonderfully complex and authentic pollo en mole negro, sporting that perfect, complex blend of sweet and spicy.

■ 3402 W. Montrose Ave. (bet. Bernard St. & Kimball Ave.)

🚇 Kedzie (Brown)

✆ (773) 539-5887 — **WEB:** www.ixcatecogrill.com

■ Dinner Tue – Sun   **PRICE:** $$

JAM

American • Neighborhood

♿

MAP: B3

Even in its new digs, Jam remains the sweetheart of brunch-o-philes who won't settle for some greasy spoon. White walls and stone tables punctuated by lime-green placemats give a gallery-like feel to the space; while a friendly welcome and open kitchen keep things homey.

Creative and refined versions of weekend favorites set this kitchen apart. For instance, French toast features brioche slices soaked in vanilla and malt-spiked custard, cooked sous vide and then caramelized in a sizzling pan. Garnished with lime leaf-whipped cream and pineapple compote, this staple is sure to cure any hangover. Eggs benedict, with house-made English muffins bested with eggs, black garlic mayo, spring onion pureé and juicy slabs of pork belly, is a thrill.

■ 2853 N. Kedzie Ave. (bet. Diversey Ave. & George St.)

🚇 Logan Square

✆ (773) 292-6011 — **WEB:** www.jamrestaurant.com

■ Lunch Thu – Tue   **PRICE:** ⊖⊖

KAI ZAN 😋
Japanese • Cozy

MAP: C5

Despite doubling its space a few years ago, Kai Zan is still the kind of place that needs a reservation well in advance. Located on an otherwise solitary stretch of Humboldt Park, the space is particularly charming and makes you feel like you are stepping into a cozy neighborhood izakaya tucked away in a remote Japanese fishing hamlet. Savvy diners book a seat at the marble sushi counter to watch chefs and twin brothers Melvin and Carlo Vizconde perform their magic up close.

The brothers turn out sophisticated, creative dishes that are decked with myriad sauces, flavors and textures. Non-traditional sushi, nigiri, yakitori, as well as classic bar bites like takoyaki and karaage are all crafted with precise details and impeccable ingredients.

▨ 2557 W. Chicago Ave. (at Rockwell St.)
𝒫 (773) 278-5776 — **WEB:** www.eatatkaizan.com
▨ Dinner Tue – Sat

PRICE: $$

LONESOME ROSE 😋
Mexican • Friendly

 ♿ ▱

MAP: C4

Lonesome Rose won't be lonely for long as it's quite easy to fall in love with her. With big windows draping its space in light all day long, this bright Humboldt Park charmer feels like it was ripped right out of a Southern California postcard—the sun's rays streaming down on bright white brick, blonde wood and a few saturated pops of color.

Brought to life by the folks behind Longman & Eagle, this kitchen's menu features thoughtfully prepared Mexican food, made in-house and impeccably fresh. Don't miss the delicious ceviche, studded with tender cubes of pineapple and pickled jalapeño. Other top contenders have included the tuna tostada, tacos, as well as street corn laced with tomatillo salsa, cotija, edible flowers and a chili "gastrique."

▨ 2101 N California Ave. (at North Point St.)
🚇 California (Blue)
𝒫 (773) 770-3414 — **WEB:** www.lonesomerose.com
▨ Lunch & dinner daily

PRICE: ☙

LONGMAN & EAGLE

Gastropub · Tavern

MAP: B3

Marked by a single ampersand over the door, Longman & Eagle is the ultimate merging of the Old World and New Order. It's where remnants of a glorious past live in harmony with chefs who prefer bandanas and beards to toques; and the cuisine remains as ambitious as ever despite the room's saloon-like feel.

Although lunch is rather limited, the kitchen remains busy at all times and the cocktail program is nothing short of stellar. Creativity is at the center of each dish, including mortadella-stuffed agnolotti served with a vibrant pea purée and savory ham broth; or a block of deliciously flavored pork jowl coupled with Brussels sprouts, pommes purée and apple jus. Distinct desserts may reveal a tart key lime pie nicely balanced by sweet coconut cream.

- 2657 N. Kedzie Ave. (at Schubert Ave.)
- Logan Square
- (773) 276-7110 — **WEB:** www.longmanandeagle.com
- Lunch & dinner daily   **PRICE: $$**

L' PATRON ⅼ◯

Mexican · Simple

MAP: B4

This local, no-frills and much-loved taqueria may have moved locations, but things remain largely the same. Signature lime-green and bright orange hues continue to decorate the interior space, which also features counter service, blaring bachata to keep you moving as you munch, and those wonderfully soft and flavorful homemade tortillas, tortas, tacos and burritos.

Ultra-fresh dishes are assembled to order, like the taco al pastor, filled with sumptuous chunks of achiote-marinated pork and topped with chopped onion and cilantro. Then a version with carne asada may be offered, packed with grilled, well-seasoned beef; while crisp tortilla chips, still warm from the fryer, are addictive companions for scooping up chunky and garlicky guacamole.

- 3749 W. Fullerton Ave. (bet. Hamlin & Ridgeway Aves.)
- (773) 799-8066 — **WEB:** N/A
- Lunch & dinner Wed – Mon   **PRICE:** ☺☺

LULA CAFE

American • Bistro

MAP: B3

This darling neighborhood staple is just as it's always been. No matter what's on the constantly evolving menu, the fresh, seasonal and original fare keeps it slammed with Logan Square locals from morning to night.

Barbecued wedges of spaghetti squash topped with Asian pear, daikon, and sesame is impossible not to finish. Nicely grilled steaks are accompanied by a tangle of blistered long beans brushed in a house XO sauce with deliciously chewy bits of dried seafood for maximum flavor. Finish with a tall wedge of double-layered carrot cake complete with crème anglaise and a luxurious spoonful of strawberry preserves on the side. Come on Monday nights for their inspired Farm Dinners and get a taste of what is to come on the regular menu.

■ 2537 N. Kedzie Ave. (off Logan Blvd.)

▥ Logan Square

℘ (773) 489-9554 — **WEB:** www.lulacafe.com

■ Lunch & dinner Wed – Mon

PRICE: $$

MI TOCAYA

Mexican • Colorful

MAP: C3

Boasting a lively, charming ambience; friendly, knowledgeable service; and a delicious menu courtesy of Chef/owner Diana Davila, Mi Tocaya is a welcome addition to the burgeoning Logan Square food scene. Bring friends, order a clever seasonal cocktail, try something from the menu and you'll no doubt leave with a renewed love for Mexican cuisine.

The short but intriguing listing of "small cravings" (antojitos) is influenced by the less-explored Aztec cuisine. Sample dishes like guisado de nopalitos, a fragrant, earthy stew with cactus, zucchini and charred chilies, served with delicious knobs of salt-dusted fried cheese curds and warm corn tortillas. But don't overlook the warm tacos, sure to transport you to the streets of Mexico City.

■ 2800 W. Logan Blvd. (at California Ave.)

▥ California (Blue)

℘ (872) 315-3947 — **WEB:** www.mitocaya.com

■ Dinner Tue – Sun

PRICE: $$

NOON-O-KABAB 🍴

Persian • Elegant

&

MAP: B1

A bustling lunch crowd appreciates the welcoming hospitality at this family-run Persian favorite in the heart of the North Side. Intricate tilework and patterned wall hangings offset the closely spaced linen-topped tables and add touches of elegance to the homey space.

Kashk-e-bademjan is a savory mash of pan-fried eggplant garnished with caramelized onions and yogurt, perfect while perusing the kebabs on the menu. Succulent, hand-formed lamb koubideh and beef tenderloin skewers are juicy and charred with a hint of spice, and vegetarian offerings like tadiq with ghormeh sabzi play up the textural contrast of crispy pan-browned saffron rice against flavorful stewed spinach. In a hurry? Head across the street to the fast-casual sis for lunch specials.

    4661 N. Kedzie Ave. (at Leland Ave.)
    Kedzie (Brown)
    (773) 279-9309 — **WEB:** www.noonokabab.com
    Lunch & dinner daily   **PRICE:** 🍴🍴

OSTERIA LANGHE 🍴

Italian • Osteria

🛱

MAP: C4

Osteria Langhe offers Logan Square a genuine taste of Italy—Piedmont, to be exact. Partners Aldo Zaninotto and Chef Cameron Grant have created a sophisticated, welcoming and contemporary space, with warm, glowing bulbs that protrude from the walls, bare wood tables and metal chairs lining the floor. Additionally, a communal table at the restaurant's entrance, is visible through its garage-like glass façade.

The regionally focused food and wine list celebrates the Italian way of eating ("slow food") with legendary Piemontese pasta like the tajarin, a plate of deliciously eggy noodles twirled around savory ragù, diced carrots and bright green parsley. Dinner specials offer great value, most notably the Trifecta Tuesday $38 prix-fixe.

    2824 W. Armitage Ave. (bet. California Ave. & Mozart St.)
    California (Blue)
    (773) 661-1582 — **WEB:** www.osterialanghe.com
    Dinner nightly   **PRICE:** $$

PARACHUTE ✿
Fusion • Colorful

♿

Husband-and-wife chef team Johnny Clark and Beverly Kim have put their little corner of Avondale on Chicago's culinary map with this hip and homey bistro. Young foodies fill the space every night, whether seated at tables lining the wooden banquette or perched along colorful stools dotting the double-sided counter that faces the open kitchen.

Though there's a distinctive Korean thread running through the menu, Parachute is a creative, open-ended endeavor at heart. Impeccably sourced ingredients from local purveyors lay the framework, but the team's brilliant application of cutting-edge techniques takes the fare to inventive heights.

Baked potato bing bread, a signature flatbread carb-bomb, is stuffed with melted scallions and bacon bits, topped with sesame and served with sour cream-butter. The regularly re-written menu has also been known to feature tender braised pork shoulder with a fermented black bean- and dried shrimp-sauce, which is then paired with ripe figs and grilled pearl onion petals. Desserts make a stellar finish. Order the patbingsu—it arrives in a glass bowl layered with condensed milk ice cream, mochi rice cakes, concord grape shaved ice, Adzuki beans and toasted rice.

■ 3500 N. Elston Ave. (at Troy St.)

☏ (773) 654-1460 — **WEB:** www.parachuterestaurant.com

■ Dinner Tue – Sat   **PRICE: $$**

PARSON'S CHICKEN & FISH

American • *Friendly*

MAP: C4

For the young professionals and new families of gentrifying Logan Square, Parson's Chicken & Fish is a lively but low-key hangout that hits all the bases. It's equally appropriate for a midday snack with the kids or a late-night munchies run, and the stay-and-play vibe extends to on-site activities like a winter ice skating rink or summer ping pong tables.

As per the name, poultry and seafood offerings are house specialties, with signature golden-fried chicken (and equally popular Negroni slushies) on many tables. An aïoli-smeared brioche bun holds a piping-hot fillet of beer-battered fish topped with crisp slaw and house hot sauce. Dessert isn't made in house, but no matter; neighboring Bang Bang Pie Shop provides daily slices of sweetness.

- 2952 W. Armitage Ave. (at Humboldt Blvd.)
- California (Blue)
- (773) 384-3333 — **WEB:** www.parsonschickenandfish.com
- Lunch & dinner daily   PRICE: $$

QUIOTE

Mexican • *Chic*

MAP: C3

Logan Square may be buzzing with Mexican restaurants, but Quiote rises above them like a brightly hued piñata. Warm and inviting, with food that satisfies from sun up to sun down, this place embodies the very essence of a neighborhood spot.

While the menu's assortment of small and large plates is meant for sharing, the kitchen aims to please and will create a typical three-course meal upon request. Expect authentic Mexican cooking with a creative twist, as evidenced by dishes such as the chorizo verde, a green-tinted pork sausage resting on smashed and griddled potatoes with sweet rings of onion and a golden raisin vinaigrette, or seasonally inspired plates like the flavorful crab tostada. As for what to drink? Three words: subterranean mezcal bar.

- 2456 N. California Ave. (at Altgeld St.)
- California (Blue)
- (312) 878-8571 — **WEB:** www.quiotechicago.com
- Lunch & dinner Wed – Mon   PRICE: $$

THE RADLER

German • Tavern

MAP: C4

With around 20 suds on tap and more than 95 bottles to sample, The Radler is everything you want in a beer hall. The restaurant may be young, but the space retains an old soul thanks to communal benches that harken back to the days of Bavarian biergartens. The enormous "Bohemian Export" beer mural that commands guests' attention is original to the building—a happy discovery during demolition. A stack of small plates on each table sends the message that everything on the menu is meant for sharing.

The haus pretzel with a mustard trio is excellent, as is the Schweinsteiger sausage. Also try the deep-golden pork loin schnitzel with bacon-braised lentils, dried Mission figs and smoky cream sauce, balanced with a light green salad and charred lemon.

- 2375 N. Milwaukee Ave. (bet. California & Fullerton Aves.)
- California (Blue)
- (773) 276-0270 — **WEB:** www.dasradler.com
- Lunch & dinner Tue – Sun   PRICE: $$

SHOKRAN MOROCCAN GRILL

Moroccan • Colorful

BYO   S

MAP: A2

Embrace Moroccan hospitality to the fullest and bone up on your Arabic at Shokran, where the country's culinary culture is displayed in a romantic setting. Nooks and crannies throughout the dining rooms offer intimacy; take a seat among the cozy cushioned banquettes and prepare to say "shokran" (thank you) repeatedly as courses come your way.

Traditional dishes offer the most authentic experience, like sweet and savory bastilla, a flaky pastry starter that's large enough to serve two, stuffed with spiced chicken and dusted with cinnamon. Famously rustic, the lamb Marrakesh tagine features a meaty bone-in shank adorned with slivers of bitter preserved lemon and surrounded by sweet peas, whole black olives and tender quartered artichoke hearts.

- 4027 W. Irving Park Rd. (bet. Keystone Ave. & Pulaski Rd.)
- Irving Park (Blue)
- (773) 427-9130 — **WEB:** www.shokranchicago.com
- Dinner Wed – Mon   PRICE: ☯

SMOQUE BBQ 😮

Barbecue • Simple

 ♿

MAP: A2

Smoque BBQ opens for lunch at 11:00 A.M., but a crowd of devotees can be found lining up for a smoky fix long before then. Once inside, peruse the chalkboard menu; then order cafeteria-style before staking your claim among the communal seating while waiting (and salivating).

The half-and-half sandwich, piled with pulled pork and brisket, is the best of both worlds, with chunky shreds of tender pork and spice-rubbed slices of pink-rimmed beef spooned with vinegary barbecue sauce. The usual side dish suspects like zingy, crisp coleslaw and deeply smoky baked beans are anything but standard here, complementing the 'cue as they should. For a sweet finish, look no further than pecan bread pudding drizzled with salted caramel-Bourbon sauce.

▦ 3800 N. Pulaski Rd. (at Grace St.)

🚇 Irving Park (Blue)

☏ (773) 545-7427 — **WEB:** www.smoquebbq.com

▦ Lunch & dinner Tue – Sun   **PRICE:** 🍽

SOL DE MEXICO 😮

Mexican • Cozy

 ♿

MAP: A3

Far more authentic than the average chips-and-salsa joint, Sol de Mexico brightens the scene and palate with a lively atmosphere (cue the mariachi music!) and delectable house specialties. Walls painted in tropical pinks, blues and oranges are a cheerful canvas for Dia de los Muertos artifacts. To sample the kitchen's skill, start with sopes surtidos "xilonen"—four molded masa cups with a variety of fillings like caramelized plantains doused in sour cream, or tender black beans topped with crumbly house-made chorizo. Then, move on to the pollo en mole manchamanteles, which translates to "tablecloth stainer." Rich and slightly bitter with a comforting nuttiness, the aptly named mahogany sauce begs to be sopped up with freshly made tortillas.

▦ 3018 N. Cicero Ave. (bet. Wellington Ave. & Nelson St.)

☏ (773) 282-4119 — **WEB:** www.soldemexicochicago.com

▦ Lunch & dinner Wed – Mon   **PRICE:** $$

STAROPOLSKA
Polish • Rustic

                                        MAP: B3

Fans of traditional Polish cooking know to proceed to this Logan Square mainstay. If a stroll past nearby Kurowski's Sausage Shop doesn't put you in the mood for some meaty, belly-busting cuisine, then one step inside this old-world sanctum certainly will.

Polish pilsners and lagers are poured at the bar and pair perfectly with the stuffed and slow-cooked plates sent out by this kitchen. Pierogies are a staple and are offered here with a variety of sweet and savory embellishments. Stuffed cabbage is a hearty delight with a meatless mushroom filling, and house specialties may include the light and tender griddled potato pancake that is folded over chunks of pork and bell pepper slices and braised in a tomato and sweet paprika sauce.

▦ 3030 N. Milwaukee Ave. (bet. Lawndale & Ridgeway Aves.)
℘ (773) 342-0779 — **WEB:** www.staropolskarestaurant.com
▦ Lunch & dinner daily   **PRICE:** ⊜⊜

TABLE, DONKEY AND STICK 🐾
Austrian • Neighborhood

🍺 ♿ 🏕   **MAP:** C4

When American comfort food just won't suffice, look to Table, Donkey and Stick for a helping of cozy Alpine fare. The rustic inn-inspired setting reflects its reputation as a gathering place where friends meet at the inviting bar or settle in at communal tables for whimsical, creative compositions.

Though the cuisine is European-influenced, ingredients from local farms make their way into many dishes. Caraway seeds spice up duck meatballs nestled among springy egg noodles with dehydrated sauerkraut and shaved salted egg yolk, and honeycomb tripe wins new fans when fried to a crisp and topped with house-made giardiniera. For a sweet take on the traditional baked good, try the pretzel-shaped puff pastry sprinkled with candied mustard seeds.

▦ 2728 W. Armitage Ave. (bet. California Ave. & North Point St.)
🚇 Western (Blue)
℘ (773) 486-8525 — **WEB:** www.tabledonkeystick.com
▦ Dinner nightly   **PRICE:** $$

WASABI ⏍〇

Japanese · *Chic*

&

MAP: C4

Who says comfort food must be consumed in humdrum digs? Certainly not Wasabi, where globe lights, sleek booths and towering windows exude modern-midcentury sophistication. Down the street from its sister restaurant, which lured patrons for years with the promise of soothing bowls of ramen, this outpost makes it easier to pop in for a quick fix—minus the lines.

Tonkatsu, shoyu, and garlic miso broths bob with springy noodles and ace ingredients, such as pork belly, a six-minute egg, wood ear mushrooms and marinated bamboo shoots. Ramen is a highlight, but it's not the only option. In fact, you may pick from a host of others like pork belly buns, dumplings and rice bowls piled with panko-crusted Berkshire pork, thinly sliced Wagyu or salmon.

▨ 2101 N. Milwaukee Ave. (at Maplewood Ave.)

▣ Western (Blue)

✆ (773) 227-8180 — **WEB:** www.wasabichicago.com

▨ Lunch & dinner daily

PRICE: ◉◉

The sun is out — let's eat alfresco! Look for ⛱.

LAKEVIEW & WRIGLEYVILLE

ROSCOE VILLAGE

Lakeview is the blanket term for the area north of Lincoln Park, including Roscoe Village and Wrigleyville (named after its iconic ball field). Keeping that in mind, enjoy a boisterous game with maximum conveniences at a Wrigley Field rooftop like **Murphy's Bleachers**, where hot dogs and hamburgers are chased down with pints of beer. When the beloved Cubs finish their season each October, don't despair, as these American summertime classics continue to shape the neighborhood's cuisine. Thanks to a large Eastern European population, a sumptuous supply of sausages and wursts can be found in a number of casual eateries or markets, including **Paulina Market**—a local institution where expected items like corned beef and lamb are offered beside more novel delights like ground venison and loin chops. This is also a hot spot among local Swedish families, who come for time-tested plates of pickled Christmas ham or even cardamom-infused sausages. Other residents may opt to sojourn to **Ann Sather**, a sweet brunch spot branded

for its baseball glove-sized cinnamon buns.

CLASSIC CHICAGO

Diners are all the craze in this neighborhood, starting with **Glenn's,** whose menu reads like a seafaring expedition with over 16 varieties of fish on offer. And between its kitchen's savory egg specialties, 30 types of cereal, and a blackboard menu that makes Egyptian tombs look brief, this is a veritable big city sort of spot and flaunts something for everyone. Similarly, the Windy City's passion for the humble hot dog is something to write home about, and Lakeview offers plenty of proof. Case in point—the dogs and burgers at **Murphy's Red Hots**, which may be simple

in presentation, but are in fact amazing to taste. And keep in mind that this location has outdoor picnic tables and no inside seating.

BAKING IN BAVARIA

Even Chicagoans can't survive on hot dogs alone. Thankfully, Lakeview has an antidote for practically every craving imaginable. Should you have a hankering for Bavarian baked goods, for instance, **Dinkel's Bakery** is right around the corner. Originally opened by a master baker from Bavaria in 1922, this family-run business (in its current locale since 1932) is renowned for faithful renditions of strudels, butterkuchen, and stollen. Their big breakfast sandwich, the Dinkel's Burglaur, may be less traditional but is just as tasty—not unlike those decadent donuts. All the items here can be purchased fresh, but they are also available frozen for shipping to lucky out-of-town fans.

FASCINATING FOOD FINDS

For a different type of high, stop by south-of-the-border

sensation, **5411 Empanadas**. This food truck-turned-storefront sells Argentinian empanadas with such inventive fillings as malbec beef or chorizo with patatas bravas. It also showcases impressive Latin sweets like alfajores to go with good, strong coffee. Connoisseurs of quality baked goods will want to pop into **Bittersweet Pastry Shop**, where luscious desserts are crafted for almost two decades now. It's a one-stop shop for everything from breads, pastries, and cupcakes, to exquisitely sculpted wedding confections. Those seeking a classic American experience should proceed to **The Roost Carolina Kitchen** for a 24-hour buttermilk-brined, hotter-than-hot take on the popular Southern fried hot chicken sandwich. Another laudation, even if it comes in buttery and sugary packages to these neighborhoods, is **City Caramels**, home to some lip-smacking treats. Settle in before making your way through Bucktown (by way of coffee-inspired caramels with chocolate-covered espresso beans); Lincoln Square (toasted hazelnuts anybody?), and Pilsen (Mexican drinking chocolate with ancho chili) along with their respective caramel and candy cuts. If savory bites are more your style, trek to **Pastoral**, commonly hailed as one of the country's top destinations for cheese. Their classic and farmstead varietals, fresh breads and olives, as well as intermittently scheduled tastings are a local treasure. An offbeat yet quirky vibe is part and parcel of Lakeview's fabric, and testament to this fact can be found at **The Flower Flat**, boasting a comforting breakfast or brunch repast in an actual flower shop. Meanwhile, **Uncommon Ground** is as much a restaurant serving three square meals a day as it is a coffee shop revered for its live music talent and performances. During the months between June and September, stop by at any time to admire their certified organic sidewalk garden before tasting its bounty on your plate, inside. And a few more blocks north, aspiring young chefs with big dreams proudly present a wholesome grab-n-go restaurant called **Real Kitchen**. Here on the menu, homestyle items like baked Amish chicken are paired with a unique and crusty pork belly sandwich to reflect each chef's take on a favored classic.

ROSCOE VILLAGE

Everyone loves a rollicking street fair, and this nabe's **Shock Top Oyster Fest** featuring an incredible music and beer selection, as well as worthy guests of honor (maybe a certain mollusk believed to have aphrodisiac qualities) certainly doesn't disappoint. Finally, die-hard dessert fiends should take note: no feast in this neighborhood is complete without a bit of sweet, so be sure to bide time at **Scooter's Frozen Custard**. Their creamy frozen offerings are made fresh daily and in a variety of flavors that are bound to delight.-

Lakeview & Wrigleyville

WELLES PARK

Sunnyside Ave.

W. Montrose Ave.

Montrose

1

W. Pensacola Ave.

Cullom

Ave.

Wolcott

Ravenswood

W.

Cullom

Ave.

Western

Leavitt

Damen

Ave.

Paulina

Berteau

Greenview

W. Berteau

🍴⭕ Kitsune

Campbell

Cho Sun Ok 🍴⭕

W. Warner Ave.

Belle

Plaine

Lincoln

Ave.

Ave.

W.

Belle

Plain

LAKEVIEW SCHOO PARK

Ashland

St.

Oakley

2

🍴⭕ Sticky Rice

W.

Irving

Park

St.

Irving Park Rd.

Ave.

REVERE PARK

Ave.

W.

Byron

St.

N.

W.

Byro

Ave.

Hoyne

Ave.

W.

Grace

St.

Paulina

LAKEVIEW

W.

Waveland

Ave.

Marshfield

Rockwell

Ave.

St.

W.

Addison

St.

Addison

W.

3

N.

N.

N.

Paulina

St.

W.

Cornelia

Ave.

St.

Paulina

W.

Roscoe

St.

Ravenswood

Ave.

N.

PARK

457

DEVRY UNIVERSITY

W.

School

St.

N.

Leavitt

Wolcott

NORTH

W.

Oakley

FELLGER PARK

Belmont

Ave.

Ashland

W. Barry

Hoyne

Ave.

N.

Western

HAMLIN PARK

Damen

Honore

Ave.

Paulina

Ave.

4

W.

Ave.

Wellington

St.

Rockwell

Ave.

N.

Clybourn

Ave.

W. Wolfram

BRANCH

W. George St.

Campbell

Elston

Logan

Blvd.

Ave.

W.

Diversey

Pkwy.

W.

Diversey

Ave.

St.

HUMBOLDT PARK & LOGAN SQUARE

5

Kennedy

90 94

Expwy.

Logan

Ave.

W.

W. Logan Blvd.

A B C

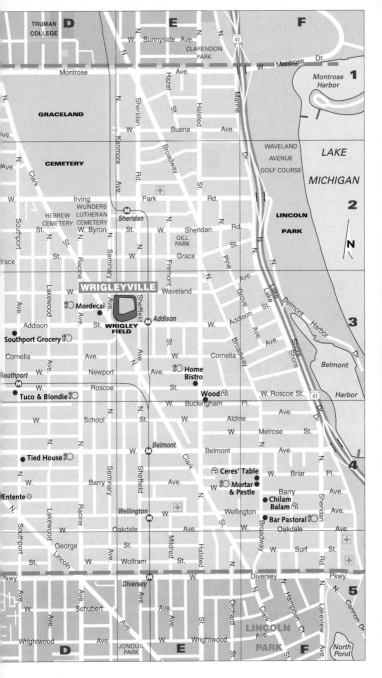

BAR PASTORAL
International • Wine bar

MAP: F4

With a cheese selection that spans the globe and charcuterie flaunting the best in the Midwest, this is a prized haunt among urbanites craving some wine with their savory eats. Subtly styled like a cave for aging, its barrel-vaulted ceilings and exposed brick walls evoke intimacy. A half-moon bar, marble-topped cheese counter and wood tables let guests gather and sample.

As expected, many dishes feature cheese, though larger and shareable plates "from the kitchen" range from simple (roasted garlic plate) to complex (rack of lamb). Thick slices of bacon-wrapped country pâté are studded with pistachios. And, a concise wine list offers unique options for coupling with cheese, of course—the raw cow's milk Kentucky Rose with onion chutney is thoroughly delicious.

■ 2947 N. Broadway (bet. Oakdale & Wellington Aves.)
▥ Wellington
✆ (773) 472-4781 — **WEB:** www.pastoralartisan.com
■ Lunch Sat – Sun Dinner nightly   PRICE: $$

CERES' TABLE
Italian • Elegant

MAP: F4

Ceres' Table continues its reign as a stylish setting for the kitchen team's rustic Italian cooking. Whether waking up with brunch, snacking at aperitivo hour or filling up at the bar with the $22 trio (pizza or pasta, beer or wine, and a dessert), there's an excuse to stop in for any occasion or budget.

Seasonal cuisine offering elegantly simple dishes made with solid skill is represented throughout the menu. Here, a wood-burning oven turns out a range of first-rate pizzas, as well as mains, like a perfectly grilled whole branzino set on a plate and topped with a heaping pile of lightly dressed salad greens and shaved radish. For more sweet simplicity, try the Tuscan torta della nonna with baby pine nuts coating a wedge of vanilla-tinged custard pie.

■ 3124 N. Broadway (bet. Barry Ave. & Briar Pl.)
▥ Belmont (Brown/Red)
✆ (773) 922-4020 — **WEB:** www.cerestable.com
■ Lunch Sun Dinner Tue – Sun   PRICE: $$

CHILAM BALAM 😊

Mexican • Cozy

BYO   S   **MAP:** F4

Chilam Balam's cozy subterranean space feels like an undiscovered hideaway, but the secret of this lively Mexican hot spot is out. Though waits can be long, the accommodating staff goes the extra mile to mix up margaritas with BYO tequila or walk guests through the rotating roster of shared plates.

Familiar favorites and seasonal specials make for a festive spread of adventurous, yet universally pleasing dishes. Flat corn tortillas form a sandwich-style enchilada, stuffed with fork-tender beef brisket and topped with crunchy strands of sweet potato slaw. Salty chorizo and green papaya tlacoyos show that opposites attract, and peanut butter empanadas—primed for dipping in Oaxacan chocolate sauce and dulce de leche—take a childhood favorite to new heights.

- 3023 N. Broadway (bet. Barry & Wellington Aves.)
- Wellington
- (773) 296-6901 — **WEB:** www.chilambalamchicago.com
- Dinner Tue – Sat   **PRICE: $$**

CHO SUN OK 🍴

Korean • Simple

BYO   **MAP:** B1

As tempted as you might be to judge this book by its brisk, unsmiling cover, don't. Instead, enter the cozy, wood-paneled den and raise that first delicious forkful to your mouth.

Take a cue from the regulars and start with galbi, a crave-worthy signature that glistens from a sweet and garlicky soy marinade and warrants good old-fashioned finger-licking. Haemul pajeon stuffed with squid and scallions is a crisp, golden-fried delight; and kimchi jjigae is a rich, bubbling and nourishing broth packed with soft tofu and tender pork. Summer calls for a taste of the bibim naengmyeon—a chilled broth floating with buckwheat noodles, veggies, Asian pear and crimson-red gochujang all tossed together for a delicious reprieve from the city's sweltering heat.

- 4200 N. Lincoln Ave. (at Berteau Ave.)
- Irving Park (Brown)
- (773) 549-5555 — **WEB:** www.chosunokrestaurant.com
- Lunch & dinner daily   **PRICE:** ⊜⊜

ENTENTE 🏵

Contemporary · Chic

&

MAP: D4

With its striking glass façade and moody interior, this lovely sanctum makes quite an impression along North Lincoln Avenue. Entente's talented team is to thank for its creative American culinary vision and the contemporary menu—designed for sharing and well worth exploring with friends—is unabashedly authentic and interesting.

The space is composed of two dining rooms: one up front with dark floors and ceilings, and another in the back with a full view of the bustling kitchen. A bar area featuring a high wall adorned with backlit wood boxes (which shelve the spirits) offers yet another spot to sample the delicious food.

Each dish delivers a remarkable mouthful, and most of the kitchen's creations are rich as well as unexpected (imagine green garbanzo hummus, paired with savory falafel, grilled apricots and pillowy flatbread tucked with fruit and nuts). Perfectly cooked pork loin arrives tender as butter, plated with cornbread purée, fragrant sweet tea jam, cornbread studded with huitlacoche, ribbons of braised collard greens and crispy pork belly. Seafood lovers will leave smitten by the green curry—dotted with poached lobster and served with pickled cucumbers and coconut flakes.

▪ 3056 N. Lincoln Ave. (bet. Barry & Wellington Aves.)

▪ Wellington

✆ (872) 206-8553 — **WEB:** www.ententechicago.com

▪ Dinner Tue – Sat

PRICE: $$$

HOME BISTRO ¡O
American • *Neighborhood*

🛋 BYO⌐   **MAP:** E3

This bistro dishes up loads of charm with a healthy dash of humor in the heart of Boystown. Flickering tealights on the closely packed bistro-style tables faintly illuminate cozy orange walls painted with food-related quotes. Chef Victor Morenz's eclectic menu picks up influences from around the globe, but each dish is consistently gratifying.

Southern meets south-of-the-border in crisp fried oyster tacos with pickled pepper remoulade. Candied kumquats and olive tapenade contrast pleasantly against buttery seared duck breast, and a cube of warm fudgy chocolate cake placed over a swipe of coconut-peanut butter is a decadent finale. Plan for an early evening if you're looking forward to a quiet meal; at peak hours, those orange walls really reverberate.

■ 3404 N. Halsted St. (at Roscoe St.)
🚇 Belmont (Brown/Red)
📞 (773) 661-0299 — **WEB:** www.homebistrochicago.com
■ Lunch Sun Dinner Tue – Sun   **PRICE:** $$

KITSUNE ¡O
Fusion • *Contemporary décor*

🛋   **MAP:** B1

Kitsune is what happens when lauded chef, Iliana Regan (of Michelin-starred Elizabeth) opens up shop in a remote corner of Lakeview. She works serious magic in this kitchen, tossing in sprinkles of Midwestern ingredients, as well as a liberal dose of wonderful wackiness with Japanese-inspired izakaya cooking. Familiar and surprising at once, the resulting dishes are immensely popular with the area's young foodies.

Sink your teeth into thick slices of wild rice and koji porridge bread spread with house-cultured butter. Then dig into their heartwarming chawanmushi, a steamed egg custard topped with sweet Jonah crab; or slurp up the shoyu ramen, a delicious tangle of stinging nettle noodles, yuzu-marinated sea beans and grilled negi in a vegan dashi broth.

■ 4229 N. Lincoln Ave. (at Hutchinson St.)
🚇 Irving Park (Brown)
📞 N/A — **WEB:** www.kitsunerestaurant.com
■ Lunch Sat – Sun Dinner Tue – Sun   **PRICE:** $$

MORDECAI

Contemporary · *Trendy*

MAP: D3

Just a baseball's throw away from Wrigley Field, this restaurant is named for legendary Cubs pitcher, Mordecai Brown. Set inside the trendy Hotel Zachary, it appeals to sophisticated diners with its stylish interior, outdoor patio and impressive Bourbon collection.

Crowd-pleasers like fried cheese curds and burgers make an appearance on the menu, but this isn't your usual ballpark bites-kind of joint. In fact, Jonah crab arancini over squid ink aïoli elevate finger food, while roasted trout with yuzu emulsion and crisp, herb-seasoned porchetta have highbrow leanings. Stuffed with caramel popcorn, Bavarian cream, and topped with crushed peanuts as well as puffed sorghum, the crackerjack donut is a delicious riff on the popular stadium snack.

■ 3632 N. Clark St. (bet. Addison St. & Patterson Ave.)
▣ Addison (Red)
✆ (773) 269-5410 — **WEB:** www.mordecaichicago.com
■ Dinner nightly   **PRICE:** $$

MORTAR & PESTLE

International · *Neighborhood*

MAP: F4

This charming neighborhood brunch spot arrives courtesy of Chefs Stephen Ross and Stephen Paul. The farmhouse-designed space is rustic, welcoming and filled with personal touches, like reclaimed wood tables and vintage stained glass windows. As if that weren't enough, the service staff is also genuinely friendly—coffee is poured the minute you sit down, and the chefs often appear to greet guests in person.

The kitchen's slogan is "globally inspired cuisine, rooted in tradition" and their globe-trotting ingredients—merguez sausage, cheese curds, romesco sauce—wind their way into a delicious array of brunchy items. Standards like eggs Benedict and French toast get sweet elevation from unexpected, upscale elements like King crab or even foie gras torchon.

■ 3108 N. Broadway (at Barry Ave.)
▣ Wellington
✆ (773) 857-2087 — **WEB:** www.mortarandpestlechicago.com
■ Lunch Wed – Mon   **PRICE:** ⌾

SOUTHPORT GROCERY 🍴

American • Simple

MAP: D3

Equal parts specialty grocery and upscale diner, this Southport Corridor hot spot draws quite a crowd. Local products and in-house goodies are stocked in the front of the narrow space, while the rear offers comfortable banquettes for a casual sit-down meal.

Breakfast is served as long as the sun shines, with options like a freshly baked and buttered English muffin stuffed with ginger-sage sausage, a vibrant orange sunny side-up egg and pepper jelly. A side of red bliss potatoes sweetens the deal, but if you're really looking for something sugary, the grilled coffee cake is a double-layered cinnamon and cream cheese delight. Craving more of your meal? You're in luck: certain menu items, denoted with an asterisk, are available for purchase up front.

■ 3552 N. Southport Ave. (bet. Addison St. & Cornelia Ave.)

▣ Southport

✆ (773) 665-0100 — **WEB:** www.southportgrocery.com

■ Lunch daily   PRICE: ⊗

STICKY RICE 🍴

Thai • Simple

BYO

MAP: A2

Sticky Rice stands out—not only for its focus on Northern Thai specialties, but also for the quality and abundance of dishes made to order. Sunny and citrus-hued, it's the kind of place where those who dare to step outside their satay-and-pad Thai comfort zone will be greatly rewarded.

Luckily, the extensive menu makes it easy to do just that. Tender egg noodles absorb the fragrant coconut curry in a bowl of kow soy that's redolent of citrusy coriander and served with pickled greens and cilantro. Duck larb is zippy and full of spice, with an unforgettable tart-and-sweet dressing. Hint: use the spot's namesake sticky rice to temper the heat while soaking up every last drop. Food is prepared to order, so speed is not worshipped at this BYOB spot.

■ 4018 N. Western Ave. (at Cuyler Ave.)

▣ Irving Park (Blue)

✆ (773) 588-0133 — **WEB:** www.stickyricethai.com

■ Lunch & dinner daily   PRICE: ⊗

TIED HOUSE
Contemporary · Trendy

MAP: D4

Talk about an entrance: a futuristic hallway spills you into this plush "house" whose vast dining room is lined with modern artwork, a marble bar and lounge. In fact, it feels like a deluxe addition to Lakeview, and is the perfect place to enjoy a meal after one of the many events at Lincoln Hall, conveniently located next door.

Chef Debbie Gold helms the contemporary American menu, and diners should start with her "bread service," which might reveal soft rye, pillowy rolls and delicately sweet oat-porridge bread. Other winners include the "breakfast" ramen studded with lamb bacon, shiitakes and sea beans. A pork pastrami melt is piled to proper Chicago heights, then topped with Gruyère, "secret sauce," as well as Brussels sprouts- and cabbage-kraut.

■ 3157 N. Southport Ave. (at Belmont Ave.)
▣ Southport
☏ (773) 697-4632 — **WEB:** www.tiedhousechicago.com
■ Lunch Sat – Sun Dinner nightly   **PRICE:** $$

TUCO & BLONDIE
American · Colorful

MAP: D3

Solid Tex-Mex fare, killer margaritas, and a soft-serve ice cream machine in the window—what's not to love about this cheerful restaurant, with its brick walls, dramatic murals and inviting outdoor courtyard complete with a huge, toasty fireplace?

Grab a seat—outside if you can swing it—and dig into a crowd-pleasing starter like the chili con queso "Bob Armstrong," basically a chili-laced cheese sauce bumped up with ground beef, guacamole and sour cream. Then move on to a mouthwatering taco trio, starring chili-braised short rib, grilled mahi mahi or chicken tinga; or the perfectly prepared steak fajitas, joined by sautéed peppers and charred jalapeño. Paired with fresh flour tortillas, cilantro rice and homemade refried beans, this is Tex-Mex nirvana.

■ 3358 N. Southport Ave. (at Roscoe St.)
▣ Southport
☏ (773) 327-8226 — **WEB:** www.tucoandblondie.com
■ Lunch & dinner daily   **PRICE:** $$

WOOD

Contemporary · *Chic*

MAP: E3

You might think everyone comes to Wood for the great music and cheeky cocktail list (Strictly Platonic, anyone?), or even the audaciously dubbed "Morning Wood" brunch on weekends. But really, it's Chef Ashlee Aubin's menu that keeps this sleek dining space packed every night. Generous portions and that irresistibly lively atmosphere (a little bit sophisticated, a little bit disco) only seal the deal.

Aubin has crafted a rotating, seasonal menu that's concise but packs a hefty punch. Imagine wood-oven flatbreads, topped with fennel sausage and wilted greens, melt-in-your-mouth steak tartare or tangles of spaghetti con vongole. Dinner on the other hand might involve a juicy bone-in pork chop, hearty cheeseburger, tender roasted chicken and seared scallops.

▨ 3335 N. Halsted St. (at Buckingham Pl.)

▥ Belmont (Brown/Red)

☏ (773) 935-9663 — **WEB:** www.woodchicago.com

▨ Lunch Sat – Sun Dinner nightly   PRICE: $$

The ✿ symbol indicates
a private dining room option.

LINCOLN PARK & OLD TOWN

The congregation of history, commerce, and nature is what makes Lincoln Park and Old Town one of Chicago's most iconic districts. Scenically situated on Lake Michigan's shore, the eponymous park offers winter-weary locals an excuse to get out. And if that isn't enticing enough, the park also keeps its patrons happy with a spectacular array of cafés, restaurants ranging from quick bites to the city's most exclusive reservations, and takeout spots offering picnic-perfect products. Populated by college grads, young families, and wealthy upstarts, as well as home to more than a handful of historic districts, museums, shopping, music venues, and the famous (not to mention, free) zoo, Lincoln Park flourishes as a much sought-after destination year-round.

DELICIOUS DINING

Wallet-happy locals and well-heeled gourmands make reservations to come here and dine at some of the most exclusive restaurants in town. But beyond just glorious white-glove dining destinations, there's more

delicious eating to be done in this area. During the weekend, these streets are jumping thanks to a combination of plays, musicals, bars, and scores of high-rises housing affluent and brash yuppies. On Wednesdays and Saturdays during the **Green City Market**, the south end of the park is transformed into hipster chef-cum-foodie central. With the aim to increase availability of top produce and to improve the link between farmers and local producers with restaurants and food organizations, this market works to educate the Windy City's young and elderly about high-quality food sourcing. (In winter it is held across the street inside the Peggy Notebaert Nature Museum).

Lincoln Park's outpost of **Floriole Café & Bakery** brought about much jubilation, and along with it, a regular fan following. In fact, the aromas wafting from freshly baked breads, pastries, and cookies never fail to tempt onlookers. For the recreational chef, **Read it & Eat** is a kitchen workshop that doubles as a fully stocked bookstore that also boasts a fantastic selection of cookbooks. Check out their calendar of food-centric events—from informative hands-on classes to drool-worthy book launches. Like many foods (Juicy Fruit, Cracker Jack, and Shredded Wheat, for example), it is said that the Chicago-style dog may have originated at the Chicago World's Fair and Columbian Exhibition in 1893. Others credit the Great Depression for its birth. Regardless of its origin, the prolific Chicago-style dog can be found at dog stalls all over the city. One such stand is **Chicago's Dog House**, offering nearby DePaul students, as well as the neighborhood, a range of classic and specialty creations. Similarly, **The Wieners Circle** is as known and loved for its delicious dogs and fries, late hours (as late as 5:00 A.M.), and intentionally rude service. Red meat fiends may choose to carry on the party at **Butcher & the Burger**

as they do their part to stay at the helm of the burger game, or linger at **Gepperth's Meat Market**, which was established in 1906 when the neighborhood was comprised of mostly Hungarian and German settlers. Old-world butchery is the dictum here with knowledge that has been passed down for generations. If prime cuts and all the trimmings come to mind, you know you've arrived at the right place.

Meanwhile the ocean's bounty can be relished in all its glory at **Half Shell**. Here, the cash-only policy has done nothing to deter crowds from consuming platters of crab legs and briny oysters. Wash down these salty treats with a cool sip from a choice selection at **Goose Island Brewery**—makers of the city's favorite local beers. Keep up this alcohol-fueled fun at **Barrelhouse Flat**, which is always hip and happening thanks to a litany of hand-crafted punches. Lincoln Park is also one of the most dog-friendly areas around, but then what else would you expect from a neighborhood named after a huge expanse of grass? Big bellies and bold palates with Fido in tow are forever filling up on artisanal goods at **Blue Door Farm Stand**. This particularly edgy grocery-cum-café also doubles as a watering hole and breakfast hot spot for lunching ladies who can be found picking at kale salads or indulging in grilled cheese sammies. If that doesn't bring a smile, the deep-fried oreos at **Racine Plumbing** or decadent popcorn from **Berco's** boutique will certainly do the trick. To keep that sugar rush going, **Cocoa + Co.** is a chocoholic's dream. This candy shop and café stocks a heavenly collection of chocolate eats and pastries from around the world, as well as comforting cups of hot cocoa and coffee. Feeling those sugar blues? Burn off the calories with a good laugh at The Second City, the country's foremost comedy club.

The Old Town quarter has a few quaint cobblestoned streets that are home to The Second City comedy scene (now with a Zanies, too, for even more laughs). Also nestled here is June's annual must-see (and must-shop) Old Town Art Fair; the Wells Street Art Fair; as well as places to rest with beers and a groovy jukebox—including the **Old Town Ale House**. Other groups may gather (for happy hour perhaps?) at **Plum Market**, which includes a coffee bar, a wine department, an apothecary; and is dedicated to proffering the very best in local and organic products. Wells Street, however, is this neighborhood's main drag, and is really where browsing should begin. Any epicurean shopping trip should also include **The Spice House** for its exotic blends, many named after local landmarks; or **Old Town Oil** for hostess gifts like infused oils and aged vinegars. Prefer a sweeter vice? **The Fudge Pot** tempts with windows of toffee, fudge, and other chocolate-y decadence. Lastly, you may not be a smoker, but the Up Down Cigar is worth a peek for its real cigar store Indian carving.

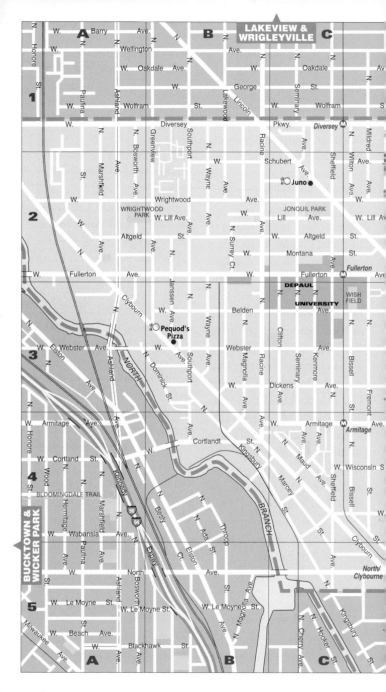

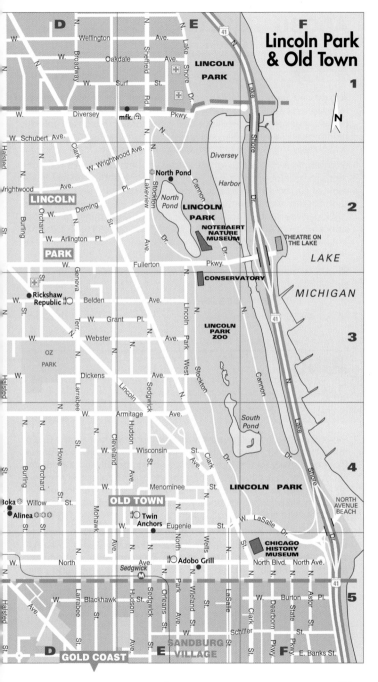

Lincoln Park & Old Town

D   **E**   **F**

N

W. Wellington Ave.
W. Oakdale Ave.
W. Surf St.
W. Diversey Pkwy.
W. Schubert Ave.
Broadway
Clark
Sheffield Ave.
Lake Shore Rd.

LINCOLN PARK

mfk.

W. Wrightwood Ave.
North Pond
Diversey
Harbor

Wrightwood Ave.
Deming
Halsted
Burling
Orchard
Clark
Pl.
Lakeview
Stockton
North Pond
Dr.

LINCOLN PARK

NOTEBAERT NATURE MUSEUM

THEATRE ON THE LAKE

W. Arlington Pl.
PARK
W. Fullerton Pkwy.
Geneva

LAKE

CONSERVATORY

Rickshaw Republic
W. Belden Ave.
W. Grant Pl.
W. Webster Ave.
Lincoln Park West
Cannon
LINCOLN PARK ZOO

MICHIGAN

OZ PARK
W. Dickens Ave.
Halsted
Larrabee
Lincoln
Sedgwick
Stockton
Dr.
South Pond

W. Armitage Ave.
Howe
Burling
Orchard
St.
Cleveland
Hudson
Wisconsin St.
Clark
Ave.

LINCOLN PARK

W. Menominee St.
Boka
Willow St.
Alinea
Mohawk

OLD TOWN

NORTH AVENUE BEACH

Twin Anchors
W. Eugenie St.
Wells
St.
North
Ave.
Adobo Grill
North Ave.
W. LaSalle Dr.

CHICAGO HISTORY MUSEUM

W. North Ave.
Sedgwick
North Blvd.
North Ave.

W. Blackhawk St.
Halsted
Larrabee
Hudson
Sedgwick St.
Orleans St.
Park Ave.
Wieland St.
LaSalle
Clark
Dearborn
State St.
Astor
Pl.
W. Burton Pl.

W. Schiller St.
SANDBURG VILLAGE
E. Banks St.

D   **GOLD COAST**   **E**

ADOBO GRILL

Mexican • *Neighborhood*

MAP: E5

A fire may have caused their move within Old Town, but their margaritas are still shaken tableside and better than ever. The space is tastefully decorated with dark wood, rich red walls hung with colorful paintings and a welcoming back patio. Many remember Adobo Grill for its tasty drinks, but the cooking is just as adept.

Guacamole is mashed to-order before your eyes, with just the right amount of jalapeños to suit your preference. Other dishes show a bit of fusion, like the ceviche de atun made with sashimi-grade tuna tossed with cucumbers, serrano chilies and creamy avocado in ginger-soy sauce. Tacos al pastor offer tender chunks of roasted pork and caramelized pineapple topping fresh corn tortillas. Desserts are pleasantly traditional.

- 215 W. North Ave. (bet. Wells & Wieland Sts.)
- Sedgwick
- (312) 266-7999 — **WEB:** www.adobogrill.com
- Lunch Sun Dinner nightly

PRICE: $$

JUNO

Japanese • *Contemporary décor*

MAP: C2

Raw fish with a side of creativity differentiates Juno from the rest of this city's sushi brethren. Inside, a rather plain and dimly lit bar up front gives way to the more contemporary, bright and airy dining room, which is a huge hit among locals looking to get all dressed-up for a night out. The menu offers cool bites like the Juno queen, a special nigiri of salmon topped with scallop and potato crunch; and hot treats like honey-glazed quail.

Chef B.K. Park's omakase must be ordered 24 hours in advance. Try cleverly spun morsels like gently torched prawn with pineapple salsa, pickled garlic oil-drizzled New Zealand King salmon, soy-marinated sea eel dabbed with ground sesame seeds and spicy octopus temaki—it's a feast well worth the extra effort.

- 2638 N. Lincoln Ave. (bet. Seminary & Sheffield Aves.)
- Diversey
- (773) 935-2000 — **WEB:** www.junosushichicago.com
- Dinner Tue – Sun

PRICE: $$$

ALINEA ✿✿✿

Contemporary • Design

✿ ⅃ 🖥 🍴

Alinea may have opened in 2005, but Chef Grant Achatz is still bursting with novel ideas. Now more than ever, this restaurant is mature, substantive, soulful and operates with an infectious confidence.

Dining here is partly theater and pure pleasure. Meals take advantage of every sense, so guests should expect scented vapors, unexpected tricks, sizzling charcoal and tableside preparations. The olfactory experience is vivid—if you keep your eyes closed, intense wafts of citrus or smoke will easily reveal what course was just served.

This chamber is sure to be packed; yet it feels more like a party than a crowd. Service is remarkably knowledgeable, attentive and engaged, thanks to a staff that brings both humor and personality to the meal. Dishes are always whimsical and sometimes experimental. While dining on a duo of squid—one as an inky sauce and another with lemon-chili butter—a bowl of oranges on the table is simultaneously filled with liquid nitrogen for a profound complementary aroma. Langoustines are compressed into a sheet of paper and then melt tableside into a superb bouillabaisse. Dessert may arrive floating on a string, as in a green apple balloon of childhood fun.

▮ 1723 N. Halsted St. (bet. North Ave. & Willow St.)

🚇 North/Clybourn

✆ (312) 867-0110 — **WEB:** www.alinearestaurant.com

▮ Dinner Wed – Sun   **PRICE: $$$$**

BOKA

Contemporary • *Elegant*

This is the kind of place where one can sink in and never leave. The three dining rooms each exude elegance with a bit of romance and quirk, thanks to walls covered in ornate escutcheons and whimsical paintings. Against these dark pebbled backgrounds, find oversized booths, banquettes and mirrored light bulbs casting funky shadows. The semi-outdoor solarium also has a living wall of moss and ferns. Servers are friendly, genuine and without a hint of pretense.

Chef Lee Wolen's modern menu is widely appealing with a Mediterranean edge. Meals are designed for guests to choose one hot and one cold appetizer, like yellowtail slices over fennel, dotted with the flavored oils and emulsions of horseradish, pistachio and Concord grape. This might be followed by campanelle strewn with chanterelles, deboned frog legs, porcini mushroom powder and pecorino. Main courses have included a graceful preparation of olive oil-poached walleye with white matsutake mushroom sabayon and roasted sunchokes.

In the same vein, dessert is an exceptionally pleasant experience. Fromage blanc beignets, for instance, are rolled in sugar, wattleseed and set over diced pear, pear sorbet and flower petals.

■ 1729 N. Halsted St. (bet. North Ave. & Willow St.)

▣ North/Clybourn

✆ (312) 337-6070 — **WEB:** www.bokachicago.com

■ Dinner nightly

PRICE: $$$

MFK. 😳
Spanish · Cozy

MAP: E1

"First we eat, then we do everything else," said M.F.K. Fisher, the food writer who serves as both the inspiration and namesake for this neighborhood darling. Thanks to large windows, whitewashed brick walls and gleaming silver-and-white tilework, the subterranean space manages to evoke a breezy seaside oasis. And with a seafood-centric menu featuring modern interpretations of Iberian-inspired plates, the food follows suit.

The ocean's bounty is showcased in simple but flavorful dishes like crispy fried prawn heads served with a nutty salbitxada sauce for dipping; and bowls of cataplana stew with fresh clams, crunchy shrimp and grilled cobia collar. A crumbly slice of Basque cake and an expertly pulled cortado end the meal on a high note.

- 432 W. Diversey Pkwy. (bet. Pine Grove Ave. & Sheridan Rd.)
- Diversey
- (773) 857-2540 — **WEB:** www.mfkrestaurant.com
- Lunch Wed – Sun Dinner nightly   **PRICE: $$**

PEQUOD'S PIZZA 🍴
Pizza · Pub

♿

MAP: B3

Ditch your diet, grab your fellow Blackhawks fans and head to this Lincoln Park stalwart for some of the best pies in town. Christened for Captain Ahab's sailing ship, Pequod's menu promises smooth sailing for sports bar noshers, featuring a lineup of shareable bar snacks such as wings and mozzarella sticks, hearty sandwiches like tender Italian beef and both thin-crust and deep-dish pan pizzas.

Grab that cutlery before digging into the buttery crust of each deep-dish pie, ringed with blackened cheese at the edges. Toppings like pepperoni, fresh garlic and crunchy sautéed onions are generously layered between tart tomato sauce and handfuls of cheese for an oozy jumble in every bite. A towering wedge of fudge cake awaits those with room for dessert.

- 2207 N. Clybourn Ave. (at Webster Ave.)
- Armitage
- (773) 327-1512 — **WEB:** www.pequodspizza.com
- Lunch & dinner daily   **PRICE:** 🍴🍴

NORTH POND ✿

Contemporary · Vintage

MAP: E2

This charming Arts and Crafts building may have started as a warming shelter for park ice skaters back in 1912, but today it is a celebratory and cozy setting that makes you want to light a fire and pop open some champagne. Exposed brick, that roaring fireplace and large windows overlooking the park and namesake pond make the rooms feel warm and pleasant.

A commitment to agriculture is clear in everything: seed packets arrive with the check and each bottle of wine has a one-dollar surcharge that is donated to charities like the Lincoln Park Conservancy or Chicago Rarities Orchard Project.

Chef Bruce Sherman's particular style seems to fly in the face of those minimalist competitors who use menus to list single components. Here, dishes are described comprehensively as a flurry of ingredients that may not always seem to fit together with great success. Try neatly trimmed Arctic char that is slow-roasted for silken texture, then served with embellishments like house-made sauerkraut, mustard seeds, candied walnuts and dauphine potatoes. A duo of strip steak and spoon-tender Porter-braised short rib arrives with pan-crisped black pepper spaetzle, Brussels sprouts and beet-apple purée.

■ 2610 N. Cannon Dr.

℘ (773) 477-5845 — **WEB:** www.northpondrestaurant.com

■ Lunch Sun Dinner Wed – Sun   **PRICE: $$$**

RICKSHAW REPUBLIC 🍴

Indonesian • *Colorful*

♿ **BYO**

The captivating flavors of Southeast Asian street food are matched by the creative design at this friendly, family-run Lincoln Avenue space. Color and pattern collide as parasols, puppets and bird cages vie for attention with abstract Indonesian wood carvings. Once the food arrives, though, the spotlight shifts to the aromatic plates.

Start with crisp martabak crêpes that hold a savory combination of beef, onions and egg. Then move on to lemongrass-braised chicken thighs in a turmeric-tinged coconut curry with sweet and spicy tamarind sambal and pickled cabbage. Surprise your palate with es cendol, a mix of coconut milk and green pandan jelly in palm sugar syrup. Finally, take home one of Mama Setiawan's homemade sambals to bring color to your cooking.

▪ 2312 N. Lincoln Ave. (bet. Belden Ave. & Childrens Plz.)

🚇 Fullerton

📞 (773) 697-4750 — **WEB:** www.rickshawrepublic.com

▪ Dinner Tue – Sun **PRICE:** 🐝🐝

TWIN ANCHORS 🍴

Barbecue • *Vintage*

🍺 🪑 🔥

MAP: E4

Within the brick walls that have housed Twin Anchors since 1932, generations have made their way across the checkerboard linoleum floor to throw a quarter in the jukebox and get saucy with a slab of their legendary ribs in one of the curved booths. Though the bar is wall-to-wall on weekends, most weekdays are low-key, with families and groups ready for a casual night out.

Fall-off-the-bone baby back ribs are the real deal, made with a sweet and spicy rub, served with their own "zesty" sauce or the newer Prohibition version, with brown sugar and a wallop of ghost-pepper heat. Classic sides like onion rings, baked beans or hearty chili round out the meal.

If there's a wait at this no-reservations spot, try the beer of the month while cooling your heels.

▪ 1655 N. Sedgwick St. (at Eugenie St.)

🚇 Sedgwick

📞 (312) 266-1616 — **WEB:** www.twinanchorsribs.com

▪ Lunch Sat – Sun Dinner nightly **PRICE:** $$

LOOP & STREETERVILLE

The relentless pace and race of Chicago's main business district is named after the "El" tracks that make a "loop" around the area. Their cacophony may be an intrinsic part of the city's soundtrack, but this neighborhood has always had a culinary resonance as well. In fact, it is one that is perpetually evolving. It wasn't that long ago that the Loop turned into no-man's land once the business crowd headed home for the night. However thanks to a revitalized Theater District, new residential high-rises, sleek hotels and student dorms, the tumbleweeds have been replaced with a buoyant dining scene, wine boutiques, and gourmet stores that stay open well past dusk. Start your culinary pilgrimage here by exploring **Block 37**, one of the city's original 58 blocks. It took decades of hard work and several political dynasties, but the block now

houses a five-story atrium with shopping, restaurants, and access to public transport. Next up: **Tesori**, a buzzing trattoria scrving hand-crafted pastas to an army of suits. Top off these savory bites with a dash of sweet at the Chicago outpost of NYC hot spot, **Magnolia Bakery**. Make sure to get in line for goodies like cupcakes and banana pudding, but for those watching their waistline, probiotic **Lifeway Kefir Shop**—with delicious frozen yogurts—is heaven on earth. And catering to the clusters of corporate crowds on the run are several fast-casual options on the Pedway level (a system of tunnels that links crucial downtown buildings underground—also a godsend during those brutal Chicago winters). For a quick grab-and-go lunch, **Hannah's Bretzel** is ace. Revered as "über sandwich makers," their version of the namesake—crafted from freshly baked German bread—features unique fillings like grass-fed sirloin mingled with nutty Gruyère, sweet vine tomatoes, and spicy horseradish aïoli. While summer brings a mélange of musical acts to

Millennium Park, Grant Park, and the Petrillo Music Shell that are just begging for a picnic, winter evenings are best spent at **The Walnut Room**. Besides all the people-watching, family-friendly vibe, and stunning Christmas décor, this Macy's gem also warms the soul with comfort foods like Mrs. Hering's Chicken Pot Pie—the recipe for which dates back to 1890. Food enthusiasts also flock to **Park Grill**, which is a full-service restaurant flanked by an ice rink in the winter. Of course, no trip to the Windy City, much less the Loop, would be complete without tasting the Italian specialties from **Vivere**—a beloved local institution that seamlessly blends formality with spirited charm in a handsome space.

TOURING & CAROUSING

Calling all sweet tooths—with flavors like candied maple bacon and pistachio-Meyer lemon, you will be hard-pressed to stop at just one donut variety at **Do-Rite**. But if dessert doesn't do it for you, enjoy eating your way through the city by way

of **Tastebud Tours'** Loop route, whose stops may include **The Berghoff**—one of the oldest known restaurants in town, with an impressive bar pouring steins of beer. Equally popular is the **Chicago Pizza Tour**, also headquartered here. From visiting restaurant kitchens, getting schooled on top ingredients, brick ovens, the science of pizza-making, and digging into deep-dish pies (naturally!), this expedition is designed to showcase the true essence behind this city's most iconic (deep) dish. During warmer months, several farmers' markets cater to the downtown droves.

These may even include the ones stationed at Federal Plaza on Tuesdays or Daley Plaza on Thursdays. Though concession carts continue to dot the streets in nearby Millennium Park, home cooks are in for a serious treat at **Mariano's**. This gourmet emporium proffers everything from gluten-free lemon bars for stiletto-clad socialites, to holiday gifts for local businesses. **Printers Row Wine Shop's** carefully curated wine selection and weekly wine tastings (every Friday at 5:00 P.M.) make it the district's go-to wine stop—intent on equipping real folks with the right amount of information. Chicago, however, also boasts its fair share of coffee connoisseurs, and tourists tired of sightseeing should rest their weary feet and opt for a pick-me-up at **Intelligentsia Coffee**—a local chain with an emphasis on direct trade. Locations can be found all over, but the **Millennium Park Coffeebar** is especially convenient and delicious.

Another one of the Windy City's biggest events is **Taste of Chicago**—a five-day summer extravaganza in Grant Park. For the last 30 years or so, the festival's never-ending maze of food booths and live music has attracted hordes of hungry diners from all over. It may be hot and crowded, but that's just part of the fun—for some!

STREETERVILLE

Bound by the strategically set Chicago River, swanky Magnificent Mile, and sparkling Lake Michigan, Streeterville is a precious locality that houses hotels and high-rises alongside offices, universities, and museums. If that doesn't scream cultural diversity, the sights and smells at Water Tower Place's **foodlife** offer indisputable proof. Located on the mezzanine floor of the shopping mall, this simple food court has been elevated to an art form. A veritable "United Nations of food courts," foodlife draws a devoted following to its 14 different kitchens that may whip up everything from hickory chicken sandwiches and deep-dish pizzas, to chicken and biscuits. Unlike other food courts, you're given a card that can be swiped at as many stalls as you choose. Once you've had your fill, bring the card to the cash register to receive your balance, and *voila*, there's just a single bill to pay! Another notable tenant of Water Tower Place is **Wow Bao** doling out some of the best steamed veggie- and meat-filled buns around. In fact, they were so popular that seven locations sprouted downtown. Hopping skyscrapers, the famous **John Hancock Center** is known to many as a "food lover's paradise." Here, bachelors in business suits come to shop for groceries with sky-high prices that match the staggering view at **Potash**

127

Markets (open to residents only). But for those whose tastes run more toward champagne and cocktails than cheeseburgers and crinkle-cut fries, there's always the Signature Room, located on the 95th floor. A sensational setting for thrilling nightcaps, this dining room also presents a fantastic brunch, lunch, dinner, and dessert menu, all of which employ some of the finest ingredients in town. While their creative cocktails may result in sticker shock, the twinkling cityscape will have you...at hello. From high-rise sips to street-level spreads, lucky locals can also be found dining with fine wine at Volare Ristorante Italiano.

ART & CULTURE

The Museum of Contemporary Art is located next to Lake Shore Park, an outdoor recreational extravaganza. Well-known for housing the world's leading collection of modern art, patrons who come here know to balance the gravitas of this setting with fresh nourishment from their in-house restaurant. But it's also the peppers and potatoes that lure foodies to the farmer's market, held at the museum every Tuesday from June through October. The world convenes at Chicago's lakefront Navy Pier for a day of exploration and eats. Showcasing lush gardens and parks in conjunction with shops and dining stalls, families usually convene at Bubba Gump Shrimp Co. for its convivial vibe and shrimp specials. Speaking of places with verve and vibe, locals looking for live music to go with their carnitas and margaritas should head on over to Jimmy Buffett's Margaritaville Bar & Grill (named after the rockstar himself). But, if you're craving a nibble in between meals, venture towards Garrett Popcorn Shops, which promises to have you hooked on such sweet-and-salty flavors as CheeseCorn and CaramelCrisp. The choices are plenty and you can even create your own tin here. Later proceed to more substantial meals that may include an all-natural Chicago-style dog (slathered with mustard, onion, relish, sport peppers, tomatoes, and celery salt) from **America's Dog & Burger**. This venerable destination showcases an impressive range of city-style creations from Dallas, Santa Fe, Atlanta, Baltimore, and Milwaukee. Of course, meat-lovers who mean business never miss **M Burger**, always buzzing with business lunchers, tourists, and shoppers alike. In fact, it should be renamed "mmm" burger simply for its juicy parcels of bacon, cheese, and secret sauce. Even calorie counters will love it here, as the "fowl mouth burger," a spicy barbecue turkey version, is nothing less than divine. For a bit more intimacy and lot more fantasy, **Sayat Nova** is supreme. Highlighting a menu of kibbeh alongside signatures like meat- and veggie-filled grape leaves bobbing in a light garlic sauce, this Middle Eastern marvel keeps its options limited but fan-base infinite.

Residents know that Chicago is big on breakfast—so big that they can even have it for dinner—maybe at Michigan Avenue's **West Egg**? This convivial café-turned-coffee corridor serves three square meals a day, but it is their breakfast specials (choose between pancakes, waffles, or other "eggcellent" dishes) that keep the joint jumping at all times. Finally, the Northwestern Memorial Hospital complex is another esteemed establishment that dominates the local landscape. Besides its top medical services, a parade of dining gems (think coffee shops and ethnic food eateries) catering to their staff and students, visitors loom large over this neighborhood— and lake.

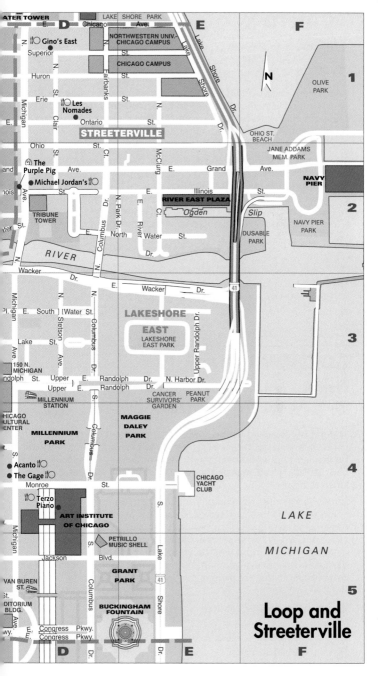

ATER TOWER
LAKE SHORE PARK
D Chicago **E** Ave.
N. 〇 Gino's East
Superior
St.
NORTHWESTERN UNIV.-
CHICAGO CAMPUS
N. St.
CHICAGO CAMPUS
Huron
Fairbanks
St.
Erie
N. St.
〇 Les Nomades
Clair
St. Clair
Ontario
St.
N.
STREETERVILLE
Ohio
St.
OHIO ST.
BEACH
JANE ADDAMS
MEM. PARK
The
Purple Pig
Ave.
McClurg
E. Grand
Ave.
**NAVY
PIER**
Michael Jordan's 〇
Illinois
St.
RIVER EAST PLAZA
E.
Ogden
Slip
NAVY PIER
PARK
TRIBUNE
TOWER
N. Park Dr.
Columbus
Dr.
N. River
Ct.
North Water
St.
DUSABLE
PARK
N.
Dr.
RIVER
Wacker
Dr.
E.
Wacker
Dr.
41
Michigan
E. South [Water St.]
E. Wacker Dr.
LAKESHORE
Stetson
Ave.
Columbus
Dr.
EAST
LAKESHORE
EAST PARK
Upper Randolph Dr.
Lake
St.
150 N.
MICHIGAN
ndolph St.
Upper
E. Randolph
Dr.
N. Harbor Dr.
Upper
E. Randolph
Dr.
MILLENNIUM
STATION
CANCER
SURVIVORS'
GARDEN
PEANUT
PARK
HICAGO
ULTURAL
ENTER
**MILLENNIUM
PARK**
Columbus
Dr.
**MAGGIE
DALEY
PARK**
Acanto 〇
The Gage 〇
S.
Monroe
St.
CHICAGO
YACHT
CLUB
〇 Terzo
Piano
**ART INSTITUTE
OF CHICAGO**
PETRILLO
MUSIC SHELL
S. Lake
LAKE
Michigan
Jackson
Blvd.
MICHIGAN
VAN BUREN
ST.
St.
DITORIUM
BLDG.
wy.
Ave.
Columbus
Dr.
**GRANT
PARK**
S.
**BUCKINGHAM
FOUNTAIN**
Lake
Shore
Dr.
41
Congress
Pkwy.
Congress
Pkwy.

Loop and
Streeterville

D **E** **F**

ACANTO

Italian • Osteria

MAP: D4

This Italian knows how to make an impression: its prime location across from Millennium Park would be a looker any day, but it goes the extra mile with style and sociability. The dining room is dressed up with angular light fixtures and orange banquettes; a luminous marble bar and matching tables lend a masculine, sophisticated vibe.

The carte's standards are as satisfying as they are spot on. Salt cod crochettes sport a golden crust and creamy filling bolstered by mashed potatoes but it's the fetching speckled earthenware dish that catches the eye. House-made rigatoni tossed with lamb ragù is well-seasoned, complex and perfect for a cold winter's night. For dessert, a fresh ricotta tart is highlighted by bittersweet orange marmalade.

■ 18 S. Michigan Ave. (bet. Madison & Monroe Sts.)
🚇 Monroe
℘ (312) 578-0763 — **WEB:** www.acantochicago.com
■ Lunch & dinner daily   **PRICE:** $$

COCHON VOLANT

French • Brasserie

MAP: C4

Though it's attached to the Hyatt, Cochon Volant is a favorite with Loop locals and sightseers alike for its timeless warmth. Round bistro tables and bentwood chairs are clustered across the mosaic-tiled floor, while a broad, marble-topped bar is bustling with patrons from lunch to happy hour.

Brasserie favorites dominate the menu, ranging from rustic French onion soup to lavish raw seafood plateaux. Steak frites is juicy and flavorsome with a tender prime cut of bavette, offered with five sauce options like a classic béarnaise or rich Roquefort. Breakfast is delicious, but for those who don't have time to sit and stay a while, the takeaway bakery lets commuters snag a pastry (cinnamon or coffee donut holes are never a bad idea) and coffee to go.

■ 100 W. Monroe St. (at Clark St.)
🚇 Monroe
℘ (312) 754-6560 — **WEB:** www.cochonvolantchicago.com
■ Lunch & dinner daily   **PRICE:** $$

EVEREST

French · Elegant

MAP: B5

Summit the historic Chicago Stock Exchange building via a private elevator to reach the sophisticated—though never outdated—scene at Everest on the 40th floor. The sunken-level dining room stays dimly lit by contemporary circular metal light fixtures, all the better to gaze admiringly at the views from the windows framing this formal space. Heavy white linens and abstract bronze sculptures adorn each table, at which smartly dressed guests take it all in.

Alsatian Chef Jean Joho keeps to French tradition on his degustation and prix-fixe menus, with nods to local ingredients among the classical techniques and pairings presented nightly. Where other chefs may feel the need to update and tweak time-honored dishes, Everest celebrates the classics. Subtle hints of ginger in a rich Gewürztraminer butter sauce complement succulent chunks of fresh and meaty Maine lobster. This may be tailed by two thick, bone-in lamb chops featuring ribbons of fat that are toothsome but never too chewy—their richness amplified by a silken spring garlic flan and bed of crisp green beans that soak up the thyme jus.

Cap it all off with tart and sweet pistachio vanilla succès dabbed with red rhubarb jam.

---

440 S. LaSalle St. (bet. Congress Pkwy. & Van Buren St.)

LaSalle/Van Buren

(312) 663-8920 — **WEB:** www.everestrestaurant.com

Dinner Tue – Sat   PRICE: $$$$

THE GAGE

Gastropub • Brasserie

MAP: D4

For more than a decade, this expansive, eclectic gastropub has catered to the Millennium Park crowds. Handsome banquettes and columns wrapped in celadon tiles lend a clubby allure, but the space's buzzy vibe never feels overwhelming. While a bar stretching half the length of the restaurant gets its fair share of happy-hour crowds, the rear dining rooms offer a more relaxed setting.

Pub classics with flair define the menu, like malt-battered cod with creamy tartar sauce and parsley-flecked thick-cut fries—a solid rendition of fish and chips. Keep it light with crunchy watercress and sugar snap pea salad with house-made burrata, or go all out with a plate of chocolate-toffee cream puffs garnished with tender cocoa-dusted marshmallows.

■ 24 S. Michigan Ave. (bet. Madison & Monroe Sts.)

▣ Madison

✆ (312) 372-4243 — **WEB:** www.thegagechicago.com

■ Lunch & dinner daily

PRICE: $$

GINO'S EAST ⅃◯

Pizza • Family

MAP: D1

Pizza pilgrims continue to make the trek to the original location of this renowned deep-dish chain, where a 45-minute wait is the norm. However, solo diners may breathe easy as they can order personal pies from a walk-up counter. The walls, scribbled with years of graffiti, are nearly as iconic as the high-walled pies themselves, whose crusts get their signature crunch from cornmeal and searing-hot metal pans with two inch-high sides.

Filled with heaps of mozzarella and toppings like the "Meaty Legend" lineup of spicy pepperoni, Italian sausage and both Canadian and regular bacon before getting sauced, it's hard for some to eat more than two wedges here. Nonconformists can of course opt for thin-crust pies, gussied up with the likes of roasted red peppers.

■ 162 E. Superior St. (bet. Michigan Ave. & St. Clair St.)

▣ Chicago (Red)

✆ (312) 266-3337 — **WEB:** www.ginoseast.com

■ Lunch & dinner daily

PRICE: $$

LES NOMADES ⅋

French • Romantic

MAP: D1

Though the casual dining movement seems unstoppable, this elegant holdout still likes to kick it old school. Here, along with classical French cuisine, guests are also treated to suited waiters and cart brigade service. In fact, this quaint two-story townhouse, set in the heart of Streeterville and decked out with throw pillow-lined banquettes, fresh-flower arrangements and an upstairs tea salon, makes for the perfect backdrop. Just past the entrance, find a small parlor and polished bar, which also doubles as a fine perch for a pre-dinner martini in an etched glass.

Come dinnertime, diners look forward to a prix-fixe menu that allows them to choose between various courses, including an ahi tart, warming mushroom soup and sweet Grand Marnier soufflé.

▨ 222 E. Ontario St. (bet. Fairbanks Ct. & St. Clair St.)
▨ Grand (Red)
℘ (312) 649-9010 — **WEB:** www.lesnomades.net
▨ Dinner Tue – Sat   PRICE: $$$$

MICHAEL JORDAN'S ⅋

Steakhouse • Contemporary décor

MAP: D2

Leave your dated 1993 Bulls jersey in the closet for a meal at this swanky steakhouse, tucked just off the lobby of the InterContinental Hotel. Leather and velvet accents telegraph an upscale vibe, and references to His Airness are subtle—from oversized sepia photographs of basketball netting to a 23-layer chocolate cake for dessert.

A glass of Amarone with a dry-aged Porterhouse is always a slam-dunk, but the kitchen also turns out pleasing modern twists on steakhouse classics. Chicago's famous Italian beef gets an upgrade with smoked ribeye and aged provolone. Similarly, the traditional wedge salad is presented as a halved small head of baby romaine, layered here with creamy Wisconsin blue cheese and thick slabs of crispy bacon.

▨ 505 N. Michigan Ave. (bet. Grand Ave. & Illinois St.)
▨ Grand (Red)
℘ (312) 321-8823 — **WEB:** www.mjshchicago.com
▨ Lunch & dinner daily   PRICE: $$$

PRIME & PROVISIONS

Steakhouse • Contemporary décor

MAP: B3

Though it would also feel at home in Las Vegas, this glitzy oversized steakhouse fits right in with its swanky Chicago riverfront neighbors. The polished, masculine interior makes its priorities clear from the get-go, showcasing a two-story wine tower and a peek into the dry-aging room under bold, barrel-vaulted ceilings and chandeliers.

A starter of chewy rosemary-sea salt monkey bread whets the palate, while rosy pink slices of slow-roasted bone-in prime rib, rubbed with a crust of fragrant herbs, take a classic hoagie to new heights. When paired with house-cut fries and creamy horseradish dip, it's a meal to rival a Porterhouse. But save room for dessert: a single-serving banana cream pie with loads of whipped cream is a whimsical final bow.

222 N. LaSalle St. (at Wacker Dr.)
Clark/Lake
(312) 726-7777 — **WEB:** www.primeandprovisions.com
Lunch Mon – Fri Dinner Mon – Sat   **PRICE:** $$$

THE PURPLE PIG

Mediterranean • Wine bar

MAP: D2

No matter the time of day, this is a fave among groups craving first-rate Mediterranean cooking with drinks and a setting to match. Everything is tasty, fun and great for sharing, so go with a posse and get a communal table all to yourselves. The bar is just as nice for solo dining, thanks to the chatty staff.

The menu covers a range of specialties from this region, including panini to a la plancha; and the kitchen turns out flavor-forward dishes that turn simple into spectacular. Need proof? Try the grilled broccoli dressed with an anchovy vinaigrette, roasted garlic and crunchy breadcrumbs. Smoked pork tongue has a noticeable smokiness with just a tinge of sweetness and is served alongside a crunchy Olivier salad with a macaroni twist.

500 N. Michigan Ave. (at Illinois St.)
Grand (Red)
(312) 464-1744 — **WEB:** www.thepurplepigchicago.com
Lunch & dinner daily   **PRICE:** $$

TERZO PIANO

Italian • *Design*

♿ ⛱ 📷 🛏

MAP: D4

Whether you're taking in the modern masterpieces at The Art Institute or simply enjoying lunch and cocktails on the sculpture-filled garden terrace, Terzo Piano is a feast for all the senses. The windowed room is mod and minimalist, allowing the artistry of the Mediterranean-influenced menu to shine brightly at each table.

With Tony Mantuano overseeing the kitchen, Italian influences find their way into many seasonal dishes. Charred tomato crème fraîche lends luxurious smokiness and a tart streak to tender chicken Milanese resting on roasted cipollini purée. And agnolotti bursting with a sweet pea-ricotta filling find savory balance with shards of crispy pancetta. As an added bonus, museum members receive a 10 percent discount on their meal.

▧ 159 E. Monroe St. (in the Art Institute of Chicago)

🚇 Monroe

✆ (312) 443-8650 — **WEB:** www.terzopianochicago.com

▧ Lunch daily Dinner Thu

PRICE: $$

Avoid the search for parking.
Look for valet 🚗.

PILSEN, UNIVERSITY VILLAGE & BRIDGEPORT

This cluster of neighborhoods packs a perfect punch, both in terms of food and sheer vitality. It lives up to every expectation and reputation, so get ready for a tour packed with literal, acoustic, and visual flavor. The Little Italy moniker applies to a stretch of Taylor Street that abuts the University (of Illinois at Chicago) Village neighborhood, and is bigger and more authentically Italian than it first appears. The streets are as stuffed with epicurean shops as an Italian beef is with meat. So, bring an appetite and try this iconic

(and messy) Chicago specialty at **Al's No. 1 Italian Beef**. After combing through the supply at **Conte Di Savoia**, an Italian grocery and takeout spot, stop for lunch at **Fontano's Subs** (locally famous for their hearty subs) or old-school **Bacchanalia**.

Brunch your way through the day by sampling a range of creative tamales (think roasted pepper-goat cheese) at **Dia De Los Tamales**, a great little spot complete with a funky décor. Speaking of south-of-the-border fun, don't miss out on the much-loved festival, **Mole de Mayo**, featuring an enticing lineup of Mexican dishes mingled with cultural events. Parched after a long day on your feet? **Mario's Italian Lemonade** is where you can seal the deal over a frozen fruit slush. Later, consider popping into **Scafuri Bakery** for a sugar refill, some biscotti, or sfogliatelle. This charming retreat has been delivering

traditional Italian sweets to the community since opening its doors in 1904. Popular for fresh-baked breads, pastries, and cookies, wedding cakes and pies are also part of their ever-changing repertoire.

UNIVERSITY VILLAGE

Like any self-respecting college "town," University Village is home to a range of toasty coffee shops. Add to that the mélange of doctors, medical students, nurses, and others working in the neighborhood hospital, and you've got a perpetually bustling vibe with great people-watching potential. On Sundays, take a break from the hustle and follow the locals to quench your thirst or feed a hunger pang at **Maxwell Street Market**. Having relocated to Desplaines Street in 2008, this sprawling bazaar welcomes over 500 vendors selling fresh produce, amazing Mexican eats, and other miscellanea. Then watch celebrity chef, Rick Bayless, as he peruses these stalls for dried chilies or epazote, while lesser Gods can be seen gorging on tacos and tostadas.

PILSEN & BRIDGEPORT

Chicagoland's massive Mexican population (more than 650,000 according to the latest U.S. Census count) has built a patchwork of regional specialties, many of which are found in the south side's residential Pilsen and Little Village neighborhoods. Pilsen is also home to the free National Museum of Mexican Art, the only Latino museum accredited by the American Alliance of Museums, as well as countless taquerias and bakeries. **Birrieria Reyes de Ocotlan** is an authentic find for tender, delicious, and flavorful goat meat folded into tacos. If that sounds too

gamey, then **Pollo Express** oozing with the tantalizing aroma of whole char-grilled chicken, is always reliable. Join their endless line for Styrofoam containers filled with creamy guacamole, adobo-rubbed chicken, and sweet empanadas. Everyone goes all out for Mexican Independence Day in September including area restaurants, while the Little Village Arts Festival packs 'em in each fall. Just as the **Pilsen Community Market** held every Sunday in the Chicago Community Bank, with its assortment of fruits and vegetables, does much to replenish the soul,

carb addicts get their fix at **Sabinas Food Products**. And for a Mexican-themed evening at home, **La Casa del Pueblo** is an exceptional supermarket that offers all things imaginable, including household, health, and beauty essentials. On the other hand, carnivores continue to gush over **Carnitas Uruapan's** pork carnitas paired with salty chicharrónes. Since 1950, **Taqueria El Milagro** has been proffering a unique taste with its cafeteria-style restaurant complete with a tamale-centric menu, as well as a store bursting with burritos and tortillas. But, lovers of all things "green" can't resist the siren call of **Simone's Bar**. This eco-friendly joint is hip and heavenly for a variety of sips. And over in Bridgeport, **Maria's Packaged Goods & Community Bar** has been a neighborhood institution in one form or another since 1939. Here, antique collectible beer cans line the space, and leftover beer bottle clusters are being constantly repurposed as chandeliers.

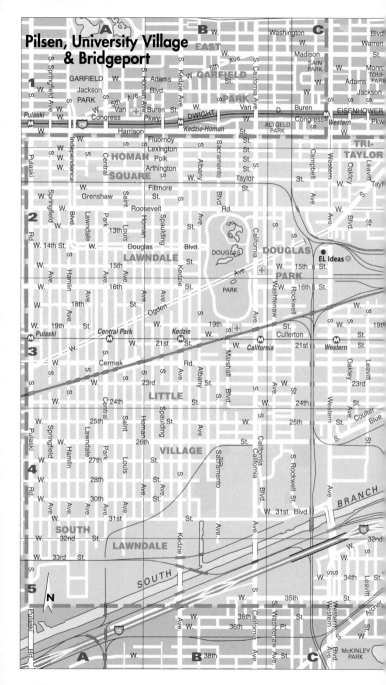

Pilsen, University Village & Bridgeport

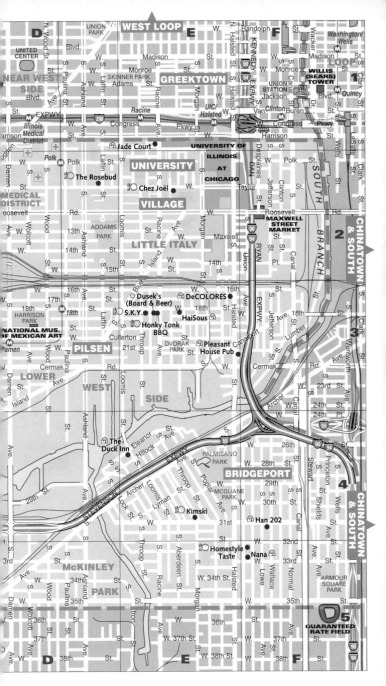

CHEZ JOËL

French • Bistro

MAP: E2

Bringing a bit of je ne sais quoi to Little Italy, Chez Joël is a stylish setting packed with expats recalling their travel stories. Here, walls gleam with ice-blue accents and windows are dressed with velvet as well as some lovely art that adds to the overall lure. A cozy bar in the back is ideal for sipping, but then get down to business by partaking in this kitchen's cuisine—classic French mingled with global effects.

For a pleasing trio of flavors, cuisses de grenouilles à la Provençale, or frogs' legs, are cooked with garlic, spinach and just the right dab of butter. Poulet aux champignons, or chicken breast, is then sautéed in a deliciously rich white wine- mushroom- and cream-sauce. Classic desserts, like the crème brûlée, are not a bad way to go.

■ 1119 W. Taylor St. (bet. Aberdeen & May Sts.)
✆ (312) 226-6479 — **WEB:** www.chezjoelbistro.com
■ Lunch Tue – Fri Dinner Tue – Sun   PRICE: **$$**

DECOLORES 🐸

Mexican • Contemporary décor

MAP: E3

This Mexican restaurant's slate-colored walls feature a beautiful rotation of work from local artists, making the walls a great conversation starter even before the delicious fare hits your table. The lovely bar is yet another bit of artistry, featuring shelves tucked around a series of metal branches; and a wonderful, colorful flower motif on the back wall. A relaxed atmosphere, warm service staff and well-made cocktails seal the deal.

At this kitchen, many of the recipes have been passed down through the family for generations. One taste of the silky mole poblano, laced over chicken and served with excellent refried beans and yellow rice, will transport you back to the motherland. Round out dinner with a wickedly good homemade cheesecake flan.

■ 1626 S. Halsted St. (bet. 16th & 17th Sts.)
✆ (312) 226-9886 — **WEB:** www.decolor.us
■ Lunch Sat – Sun Dinner Tue – Sun   PRICE: **$$**

THE DUCK INN 🦆

Gastropub • Trendy

MAP: E4

Head to the Bridgeport warehouses, where this stylish, modern tavern—helmed by Executive Chef Kris Delee—feels like a diamond in the rough. Then make your way past the buzzy bar (pouring heady cocktails) to a semi-open kitchen, which is in full view of the decorous dining room, featuring wood tables and mid-century seats.

The cuisine may be coined as «working-class fine dining,» but there is nothing lowbrow about this menu, which unveils a focused but diverse selection of small plates and mains. Japanese barbecue sauce and sesame seeds are the crowning touch to duck wings, while foie gras mousse with celery fronds and brioche is a study in fine flavors and textures. Of course, regulars know to save room for the Chicago-style duck fat dog.

- 2701 S. Eleanor St. (at Loomis St.)
- ✆ (312) 724-8811 — **WEB:** www.theduckinnchicago.com
- Lunch Sat – Sun Dinner Tue – Sun   **PRICE:** $$

HAISOUS 🦆

Vietnamese • Contemporary décor

MAP: E3

This passion project of Chef Thai Dang and wife, Danielle, offers refined Vietnamese cuisine in a plum setting. The menu, divided into five sections, is filled with wonderful, lesser-known (and possibly unexpected) dishes you won't want to miss. The restaurant offers many seating options: an open kitchen fringed with comfy seats; a bar area for cocktails and perhaps an order of those famous chicken wings; as well as two dining rooms, one with communal seating. Don't leave without sampling the goi vit (duck salad); cánh gà chiên (chicken wings with fish sauce, garlic and chili); or eggplant and octopus, laced with coconut cream and fried shallots.

For street food, specialty coffee and quenching cocktails, visit their next-door coffee shop, Cà Phê Đá.

- 1800 S. Carpenter Ave. (at 18th St.)
- 🚇 18th
- ✆ (312) 702-1303 — **WEB:** www.haisous.com
- Lunch Sat – Sun Dinner Mon – Sat   **PRICE:** $$

DUSEK'S (BOARD & BEER) ❁

Gastropub • Tavern

On the one hand, Dusek's is simply a great gastropub, serving food that is as comforting and down-to earth as one of their wood fire-roasted pretzels, tucked with gooey cheese and hot beer mustard. On the other hand, this is just the place to meet friends or grab a bite before heading to a concert at Thalia Music Hall, located next door.

The fact that this spot is named for the man who founded the original venue back in 1892 shows the importance of this connection—those in-the-know are usually headed here before or after a show. The space seems dark and moody, but everyone is having a rollicking good time. The front room feels more like a tavern; the back is a dining room warmed by the wood-burning ovens. Yet both share that same convivial ambience and superb service. Menu pleasers include chicken fried rabbit, tender and crackling like few other fried birds, on a bed of hoppin' John risotto flecked with charred okra for a homey, smoky side. Warm, soaked in rum, and hiding a mound of mascarpone with cocoa nibs, the tiramisu cruller is intensely good.

The craft beer selection is terrific, with mostly local varieties, so ask your server for pairing suggestions and you won't go wrong.

📍 1227 W. 18th St. (at Allport St.)

🚇 18th

📞 (312) 526-3851 — **WEB:** www.dusekschicago.com

🍴 Lunch & dinner daily

PRICE: $$

EL IDEAS ❀

Contemporary · Intimate

BYO

Dining here feels like attending an underground dinner party prepared by a merry band of misfit cooks in Chef Phillip Foss' home (he lives right upstairs). There is one seating, everyone is served at the same time and meals are prepaid so guests can linger or leave at their leisure.

The fact that the restaurant resembles a test kitchen is heightened when guests are told to manage their BYO beverages themselves and cooks deliver dishes to your table. Don't worry—they turn the music down so you can hear each description. Yet this is all part of the show; it's a fun, friendly, totally unique experience.

The cuisine follows suit and works wonders by pushing—if not completely disregarding—the traditional boundaries of cooking. Breaking barriers is par for the course: a croquette filled with Caesar dressing set on strips of romaine is to be eaten by licking the plate. Outlandish surprises include a hibiscus-cured salmon with aquachile sorbet, avocado crema and hibiscus gel with a dense chip. And then there is the brilliantly fun French fries and ice cream course, which is designed to look like a milkshake and made in part with a hot potato-leek soup. Once you've had it, you won't forget it.

▦ 2419 W. 14th St. (at Western Ave.)

▣ Western (Pink)

✆ (312) 226-8144 — **WEB:** www.elideas.com

▦ Dinner Tue – Sat   PRICE: $$$$

HAN 202 😊

Asian • *Contemporary décor*

 ♿ BYO

MAP: F4

Near Guaranteed Rate Field, this is the perfect spot to stop for an early meal before a White Sox game. The dining room feels polished and sophisticated, with leather-backed seats, large windows, and contemporary artwork.

The menu follows suit with food that is also an elegant departure from expectation, with cooking that is more Asian than specifically Chinese. The prix-fixe menu supplements may only be a few dollars more, but are well worth it. Diver scallops are wildly pristine and delicious, pan-seared and served with red beet and smoked yellow pepper purées over white chocolate sabayon jus. The plump bone-in rack of lamb is wonderful, as is its bonito plum sauce deeply flavored with lavender, mustard seeds and Sichuan pepper.

◻ 605 W. 31st St. (bet. Lowe Ave. & Wallace St.)

✆ (312) 949-1314 — **WEB:** www.han202.com

◻ Dinner Tue – Sun   **PRICE:** $$

HOMESTYLE TASTE 🍴

Chinese • *Simple*

 ♿ BYO

MAP: F5

For even more adventurous fare than spicy Sichuan lamb or dim sum, look no further than this family-run favorite. Though the lengthy menu offers plenty of usual suspects (think scallion pancakes and mapo tofu), it's also chock-full of Chinese dishes that will make any offal lover's day.

Thin slices of lamb kidney are stir-fried, their mild flavor boosted by copious amounts of cumin and red chilies. Then, a sweet and sour sauce offsets the funky flavor of quick-fried intestine, tripe and liver; while pickled cabbage and pork meatball soup, boosted by tofu and noodles, is a welcome warmer on cold days. The service is friendly and amenable, so don't be afraid to specify your preferred meat or ask for chili oil to amplify the heat quotient.

◻ 3205 S. Halsted St. (bet. 32nd & 33rd Sts.)

✆ (312) 949-9328 — **WEB:** N/A

◻ Lunch & dinner daily   **PRICE:** ☜

HONKY TONK BBQ 🍴⭘
Barbecue · Simple

MAP: E3

A rousing success since it opened in 2007, Honky Tonk BBQ serves up live music and award-winning Memphis-style treats on the southwest side of the city. Though the rollicking bar up front takes its cues from a swinging Wild West saloon, the rear dining room offers a more sedate—though still eclectic—setting for sipping on house cocktails and chowing down on sensational smoked meats.

You'll need two hands to hold homemade empanadas stuffed with combinations like Manchego and shiitake mushrooms, and extra cottony white bread to soak up the juices of bone-in, wood-smoked chicken. Brisket chili is even more robust with a scoop of creamy mac and cheese. And if you're still hungry, soda floats with Bridgeport-made Filbert's root beer are the cherry on top.

- 1800 S. Racine Ave. (at 18th St.)
- 18th
- (312) 226-7427 — **WEB:** www.honkytonkbbqchicago.com
- Dinner Tue – Sun   **PRICE: $$**

JADE COURT 😀
Chinese · Neighborhood

MAP: E1

Its location is a bit out of the way (unless you're a student at UIC) and its digs may leave much to be desired, but Jade Court is certainly worth the trek. The same father-daughter team that once owned Phoenix in nearby Chinatown now runs this Cantonese kitchen.

The large carte features an impressive variety of dim sum and casseroles; while blazing-hot woks turn out black bean and garlic stir-fries as well as sizzling hot plates that arrive brimming with seafood. And although most dishes come as small portions, they can still feed a group at a fraction of the price. Think of honey-glazed barbecue pork that glistens with just the right amount of fat; pan-fried noodles layered with tender beef strips; or Chinese broccoli boasting that perfect crunch.

- 626 S. Racine Ave. (at Flournoy St.)
- Racine
- (312) 929-4828 — **WEB:** www.jadecourtchicago.com
- Lunch & dinner Wed – Mon   **PRICE:** ⊖⊖

KIMSKI

Fusion • Minimalist

MAP: E4

This long-awaited development in Bridgeport, connected to the popular Maria's Packaged Goods & Community Bar, serves up deliciousness and fun in equal parts. Think: a quirky Korean-Polish fusion menu; daily mish-mash specials; and T-shirts as well as fireball sauces to take home. All the food can be ordered at the counter to-go, but do yourself a favor and make your way to the open industrial dining space or large patio to enjoy the jamming bar and some live music with your meal.

Everything at Kimski is truly unique. Try the homemade smoked sausage with soju mustard, kraut-chi (kimchi and kraut) and scallions tucked into a soft roll; or the kopo wangs, organic chicken wings slathered in a sweet-spicy AP sauce, laced with sesame seeds and scallions.

 960 W. 31st St. (bet. Farrell & Keeley Sts.)
 (773) 890-0588 — **WEB:** www.kimskichicago.com
 Lunch Sun Dinner Tue – Sun   **PRICE:** 🥜🥜

NANA 😀

American • Family

MAP: F5

Nana Solis is the matriarch of this family-run Bridgeport favorite, whose visible kitchen and two dining rooms (one less formal) seem to be perpetually humming. A devoted breakfast crowd takes up residence at the coffee "bar" and butcher-block tables each day, often perusing the marvelous modern artwork—hung on the walls and usually for sale.

Locally sourced and organic are the guiding principles behind every ingredient here, which is given a bold Latin American bent. Avocado batons are tossed in panko, then flash-fried for a crispy exterior and creamy center. Another staple among the "Nanadicts" is the eggs Benedict with chorizo, corn pupusas and poblano cream. Sunday nights feature family-style fried chicken dinners fit for groups with larger appetites.

3267 S. Halsted St. (at 33rd St.)
(312) 929-2486 — **WEB:** www.nanaorganic.com
Lunch daily Dinner Wed – Sun   **PRICE:** $$

PLEASANT HOUSE PUB

Gastropub • Neighborhood

🍺 ♿ 🪑 🛋️   **MAP:** E3

Classic English pies may be the specialty of this house, but don't let that inspire visions of chintz and tea cozies—the interior here is decidedly modern, with marble-topped tables and hand-crafted pottery.

But the crowds come for the pies, and for good reason—they're fabulous. The crust is flaky and buttery, and the inside, hearty and satisfying. Dig into the steak and ale, with its beef stew filling and side of minty peas, gravy and mashed potatoes, and you'll be hunting for every last crumb. The comfort food hits also keep on coming, from rarebit mac and cheese with Trooper Ale cheese sauce, to fish and chips on Fridays. Of course, with much of the seasonal greens from local farms, rest assured that even a simple salad will be a revelation.

▨ 2119 S. Halstead Ave. (at 21st St.)
✆ (773) 523-7437 — **WEB:** www.pleasanthousepub.com
▨ Lunch & dinner Tue – Sun   **PRICE:** $$

THE ROSEBUD 🍴

Italian • Family

♿ 🍽️ 🧼   **MAP:** D2

The Rosebud holds its own among the brass of University Village's Italian thoroughfare. The original location of what is now an extended family of restaurants throughout Chicagoland, it's nothing if not classic with its red neon sign, dark carved wood and cool but accommodating waitstaff.

Italian wedding soup brings comfort with tiny, moist meatballs, escarole and acini di pepe simmered in broth; while sweet sausage chunks, caramelized onions and a garlicky white wine sauce make chicken giambotta a satisfying choice. Loyal patrons crowd around white tablecloths for platters of their favorite chicken parmesan or linguine topped with a mountain of clams. Dessert is not to be missed either: a single slice of carrot cake will gratify the whole table.

▨ 1500 W. Taylor St. (at Laflin St.)
🚇 Polk
✆ (312) 942-1117 — **WEB:** www.rosebudrestaurants.com
▨ Lunch & dinner daily   **PRICE:** $$

S.K.Y.

Contemporary • Chic

Chef/owner Stephen Gillanders, formerly of Intro, rocks out all on his own at S.K.Y. The moniker strings together his wife's initials, though with his ambitious Asian-accented cooking, it could easily double as a descriptor.

The slightly motley menu—featuring everything from cornbread madeleines, foie gras-bibimbap and sashimi with black sesame ponzu, to a Thai steak salad, tomato panzanella and sea bass with wasabi—matches the cool, contemporary space. Crackling beef short rib marries the sweet-spicy tang of gochujang with the crunch of corn, tomato and edamame succotash in a basil-butter sauce. The aptly named tropical dessert pairs frozen yogurt and coconut fluff studded with freeze-dried raspberries, mango and kiwi for a first-rate finish.

- 1239 W. 18th St. (at Allport St.)
- 18th
- (312) 846-1077 — **WEB:** www.skyrestaurantchicago.com
- Lunch Sat – Sun Dinner Wed – Sun   **PRICE: $$**

RIVER NORTH

BEYOND THE
ORDINARY

Urban, picture-perfect, and always-happening River North not only edges the Magnificent Mile, but is also located north of the Chicago River, just across the bridge from the Loop. Once packed with factories and warehouses, today this capital of commercialization is the ultimate landing place for art galleries, well-known restaurants, swanky shopping, and a hopping nightlife. Thanks to all this versatility, the area attracts literally everybody—from lunching ladies and entrepreneurs, to tour bus-style visitors. Tourists are sure to stop by, if only to admire how even mammoth chain restaurants ooze a particular charm here. River North is also home to the original **Portillo's**, a hot dog, burger, and beer favorite, whose giant exterior belies its efficient service and better-than-expected food. When it comes to size, few buildings can rival **Merchandise Mart** (so large it once had its own ZIP code), known for its retail stores, drool-worthy kitchen showrooms, and two great food shops. **Artisan Cellar** is one such gem where in addition to boutique wines

and cheeses, you can also purchase Katherine Anne Confections' fresh cream caramels. Locals also adore and routinely frequent **The Chopping Block** for its expertly taught themed cooking courses; updated, well-edited wine selections; and sparkling knife collection.

From trends to legends, **Carson's** is a barbecue institution. This squat brick box has no windows, but is just the kind of place where wise guys like to do business— with a bib on of course! This old-school treasure features framed pictures of every local celebrity, who can also be seen gracing the walls at seafood superstar, **Shaw's Crab House**. Their nostalgic bar and dining room is dotted with stainless steel bowls to collect the shells from the multitude of bottom-dwellers on offer. Crab is always available naturally, but selections spin with the season. For those who aren't down with seafood in any form, this kitchen turns out a few prime steaks as well. Combat the bitter-cold winters and warm your soul with hearty food and easy elegance at **Lawry's Prime Rib** in the 1890's McCormick Mansion. Inside, the opulent dining room covers all the bases— from prime rib dinners to seafood signatures. But true carnivores who like their meat and potatoes done in grand style will find deep comfort in **Smith & Wollensky's** elaborate carte. Another nationwide chain, **Fleming's Prime Steakhouse & Wine Bar** is as well-regarded and recognizable as the aromas wafting from **Bow Truss Coffee Roasters**, where busy commuters pop in for a robust espresso. Don't forget to indulge your dessert dreams at **Firecakes Donuts** where coconut cream-filled buns may be chased down by piping-hot chocolate bobbing with soft marshmallows. The Windy City's donut craze then carries on at **Doughnut Vault**, brought to you by restaurateur Brendan Sodikoff, who appears to have the Midas touch with this morning fried dough.

Formerly the location for the infamous Cabrini-Green government housing, today **Chicago Lights: Urban Farm** showcases organic produce, nutritional education, and workforce training, thereby elevating the level of economic opportunities available to this vibrant community. On the other hand, **Eataly** is an impressive ode to Italian food, employing a massive workforce. This gourmet emporium may present the same delicacies as its New York City flagship location, but the Nutella (counter) with its mouthwatering selection is bound to have masses returning for more.

DEEP-DISH DELIGHTS

Thanks to its wide-ranging and diverse community, River North is also a great destination for a number of food genres, including the local phenomenon of deep-dish pizza. With a doughy crust cradling abundant cheese, flavorful sauce, and a spectrum of other toppings, some may say this is closer to a casserole or "hot dish" than an Italian-style pizza. Either

way, these pies take a while to craft, so be prepared to wait wherever you go. **Pizzeria Uno** (or sister **Pizzeria Due**), and **Giordano's** are some of the best-known pie makers in town. And if a little indigestion isn't a concern, follow up these decadent delights with yet another local specialty, namely the Italian beef. At **Mr. Beef's**, these "parcels" resemble a messy, yet super-addictive French dip, wrapping thinly sliced beef with hot or sweet peppers on a hoagie. If you order it "wet," both the meat and bread will be dipped in pan juices. You could also add cheese, but hey, this isn't Philly!

Distinguished by day, River North pumps up the volume at night with sleek cocktail lounges, night clubs, and Irish bars. Some may slip into **Three Dots and a Dash**, a retro, tiki-inspired hot spot featuring some of the city's most well-regarded mixologists; while others looking for a more rootin'-tootin' good time, should stop by during happy hour at **Green Door Tavern**, which gets its name from the fact that its colored front told Prohibition-era customers where to enter for a drink. To appreciate what all the fuss is about, order either the "famous corned beef sandwich" or even the "legend burger" and you will leave with a smile.

River North

A B C

1

N. Hudson Ave.

W. Institute Pl.

N. N. Chicago Ave. M Chicago

W. Chicago Sedgwick Orleans Franklin ● Farmhouse

N. N. St.

W. Superior St.

N. Kingsbury Hudson ● Prosec

W. Huron

N. Ave. St. St. St. ● The
Franklin
Room

2

St. W. Erie St.

ERIE PARK

NORTH

W. Ontario St.

N.

Kennedy Expwy.

W.

BUCKTOWN &
WICKER PARK

GT F
& Oys

3

W. Grand Ave. W.

N. 1st N.

Canal Kingsbury Franklin

Canal N. Clinton St. W. Illinc

St.

BRANCH

W. Hubbard St. St.

Orleans ● Bavette's Ba
& Boeuf

N. Kinzie St. ● Gilt Bar

St. Merchandise I

4

N. MERCHANDISE
MART

W. Canal St.

Jefferson Merchandise Mart Plz.

WEST LOOP

Clinton WOLF CHICAG
POINT

W. Fulton St. Wack

N.

Franklin

5

N

W. St. St. M W.

W. Lake Clinton St. St.

A B C

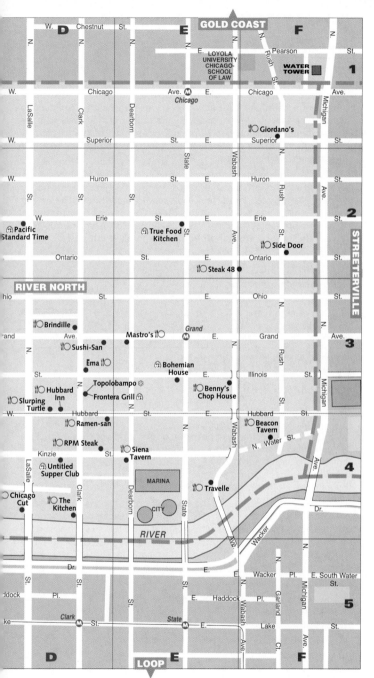

GOLD COAST

W. **D** Chestnut St. **E** N.
N. N. Pearson St.
Rush St.
LOYOLA
UNIVERSITY
CHICAGO-
SCHOOL
OF LAW
WATER
TOWER **1**

W. Chicago Ave. Ⓜ E. Chicago Ave.
Chicago
LaSalle Clark Dearborn
W. Superior St. E. Superior St.
🍴◯ Giordano's

W. Huron St. E. Huron St.
State
St. St. St.
Wabash
Rush
W. Erie St. E. Erie St. **2**

🏛 **Pacific** 🏛 True Food
Standard Time Kitchen Ave.
🍴◯ Side Door

Ontario St. E. Ontario St.
🍴◯ Steak 48 ●

RIVER NORTH

hio St. E. Ohio St.

🍴◯ Brindille ● N.
and Ave. Mastro's 🍴◯ *Grand* Ⓜ E. Grand Ave. **3**
🍴◯ Sushi-San
Rush
Ema 🍴◯
St. 🍴◯ Bohemian
House E. Illinois St.
Topolobampo ✿
🍴◯ Hubbard Frontera Grill 🍴 🍴◯ Benny's Michigan
Inn Chop House
🍴◯ Slurping Hubbard St. E. Hubbard St.
Turtle ● 🍴◯ Beacon
🍴◯ Ramen-san Tavern
N. Water St.
🍴◯ RPM Steak
Kinzie 🍴◯ Siena **4**
🏛 Untitled Tavern
Supper Club
MARINA
◯ Chicago 🍴◯ The CITY 🍴◯ Travelle
Cut Kitchen Wacker
RIVER Dr.

Dr.
E. Wacker Pl. E. South Water
St.
St. St. E. Haddock
ddock Pl. Pl. Garland Michigan **5**
ke *Clark* Ⓜ St. *State* Ⓜ E. Lake St.

D **E** **F**
LOOP

STREETERVILLE

BAVETTE'S BAR & BOEUF

Steakhouse • *Brasserie*

MAP: C4

With a sultry jazz soundtrack and speakeasy ambience, this swanky destination is unfailingly packed every evening with a boisterous crowd. The feel inside may be dark and loud, but that only adds to the bonhomie of the chic and cavernous den, outfitted with exposed brick walls, mismatched dangling light fixtures and tobacco-brown Chesterfield-style sofas.

Steakhouse and raw bar standards dominate the menu. Most steaks are wet-aged and though some may prefer more funk, the cuts are expertly broiled. Perfectly rendered steak frites served with a buttery béarnaise sauce is a great way to go. But, the kitchen deserves praise for other, more unexpected options like fresh-baked crab cake with remoulade; or creamy short rib stroganoff bobbing with hand-cut pasta.

218 W. Kinzie St. (bet. Franklin & Wells Sts.)

Merchandise Mart

✆ (312) 624-8154 — **WEB:** www.bavetteschicago.com

Dinner nightly

PRICE: $$$$

BEACON TAVERN

American • *Contemporary décor*

MAP: F4

Need a place to recharge in between bouts of power shopping? This all-American gastropub, hidden in plain sight right off the Magnificent Mile, is just your spot. Sink in to one of their plush green velvet banquettes for a sip and a snack in this gorgeous space—dominated by an open kitchen with a mesmerizing flurry of activity.

From its dark wood tables to the low lighting, this scene is definitely a luxe one, while the well-executed seafood treats flaunt a rustic sort of refinement. Fortify yourself with excellent small dishes such as shrimp toast or yellowfin tuna tartare. Pan-seared sea bass over a creamy butternut squash purée shows off a familiar flair, and if the banoffee pie is on offer, order it. After all, shopping is a serious calorie burn.

405 N. Wabash Ave. (bet. Michigan & Wabash Aves.)

Grand (Red)

✆ (312) 955-4226 — **WEB:** www.beacontavern.com

Lunch & dinner daily

PRICE: $$

BENNY'S CHOP HOUSE

Steakhouse • Elegant

MAP: E3

Old-school service meets modern elegance at Benny's Chop House. A far cry from the clubby, masculine steakhouses of yesteryear and just a stone's throw from the Magnificent Mile, this expansive but welcoming space goes for understated glamour, with tasteful inlaid wood and burgundy columns offset by natural stone walls, white birch branches, and a marble bar.

Though Benny's steaks are the draw, those prime cuts of filet mignon and ribeye are matched by seafood like a simply roasted bone-in halibut fillet and classic raw bar towers, along with a variety of homey pastas and refreshing salads. A trio of sliders featuring mini portions of Benny's burger, crab cake and sliced filet with horseradish cream elevates the idea of bar snacks to new heights.

▦ 444 N. Wabash Ave. (bet. Hubbard & Illinois Sts.)

▦ Grand (Red)

✆ (312) 626-2444 — **WEB:** www.bennyschophouse.com

▦ Lunch & dinner daily   **PRICE: $$$**

BOHEMIAN HOUSE 😊

Eastern European • Elegant

MAP: E3

This wickedly stylish "house" is exactly what River North needed to shake it up—a truly unique restaurant serving delicious Czech, Austrian and Hungarian cuisines. The stunning beer hall-meets-art nouveau space (with reclaimed wood beams, tiles arching over a semi-open kitchen, sky-blue leather couches and Persian rugs) is worth a visit alone. No detail is overlooked.

Delightfully, the food delivers on all points and is just as pretty to look at. Don't miss the open-faced schnitzel sandwich, highlighting pork over apple and kohlrabi slaw, aged Gouda, a fried egg and coarse mustard. Also a must do? The warm blueberry kolacky, which is a classic Czech cookie filled with blueberry coulis and served with lemon curd as well as blueberry-sour cream ice cream.

▦ 11 W. Illinois St. (bet. Dearborn & State Sts.)

▦ Grand (Red)

✆ (312) 955-0439 — **WEB:** www.bohochicago.com

▦ Lunch Fri – Sun Dinner Tue – Sun   **PRICE: $$**

BRINDILLE 🍴

French • Chic

MAP: D3

This posh bistro is clearly visible to passersby thanks to its large windows and distinctive signage. Hushed and intimate inside, the dining room is awash with a palette of soothing greys and dressed up with herringbone floors along with black-and-white photography. Servers may be casually dressed, but are attentive and engaging.

Brindille's menu bears a strong Parisian accent influenced by the chef's love for French cuisine. Roasted chestnuts are whirled into a creamy soup and poured over compressed apple, wild mushrooms and puffed rice. Spot-on Dover sole meunière is plated with a purée of watercress and golden-crisp pommes rissolées. And for dessert, preserved cherries are just one option to fill the baked-to-order almond clafoutis.

- 534 N. Clark St. (bet. Grand Ave. & Ohio St.)
- Grand (Red)
- (312) 595-1616 — **WEB:** www.brindille-chicago.com
- Dinner Mon – Sat   **PRICE: $$$$**

CHICAGO CUT 🍴

Steakhouse • Elegant

MAP: D4

Chicago Cut is a steakhouse perfectly suited for the City of the Big Shoulders. This finely tailored locale bustles day and night, thanks to wraparound windows along the riverfront, sumptuous red leather furnishings, warm wood trim and a crackerjack service team cementing its steakhouse vibe.

Non-meat entrées include cedar-planked salmon with a sriracha-honey glaze, but make no mistake: beef is boss here. Prime steaks, butchered and dry-aged in-house for 35 days, get just the right amount of time under the flame, as is the case with the perfectly cooked-to-order Porterhouse—pre-sliced and plated for each guest. Sides are a must and should include the dome of hashbrowns, creamed spinach redolent of nutmeg or tender stalks of grilled asparagus.

- 300 N. LaSalle St. (at Wacker Dr.)
- Merchandise Mart
- (312) 329-1800 — **WEB:** www.chicagocutsteakhouse.com
- Lunch & dinner daily   **PRICE: $$$**

ĒMA

Mediterranean • *Contemporary décor*

MAP: D3

Cross the threshold into this breezy, elegant space—all whitewashed brick, wood-slat windows and lush greenery—and prepare to be transported to the shores of the Adriatic.

The menu boasts an array of fresh, wholesome Greek and Middle Eastern dishes, like a smoky charred eggplant spread, tempting cold mezzes and a variety of kebabs. And it should come as no surprise that these items taste as though they were prepared in a cozy home kitchen, as ēma translates to "mother" in Hebrew. Dig into the lamb and beef kefta, a plate of perfectly grilled, skewered meat served alongside zhoug, a spicy herb and chile pepper relish. Then cool off with a few spoonfuls of delightfully tart frozen yogurt before booking your return ticket home to the Midwest.

- 74 W. Illinois St. (at Clark St.)
- Grand (Red)
- (312) 527-5586 — **WEB:** www.emachicago.com
- Lunch & dinner daily   **PRICE: $$**

FARMHOUSE

Gastropub • *Bistro*

MAP: C1

Like shaking the hand of your local farmer, grab the pitchfork door handles of Farmhouse and you'll be almost as close to the source of your food. Much of the décor is salvaged and much of the menu is procured right from the Midwest. From Indiana chicken to Michigan wine, local is more than a buzzword here. Exposed brick, rough-hewn wood and filament bulbs make it the quintessential modern tavern.

Highlights of the harvest headline each course. Whole-grain mustard dresses up a vibrant (and requisite) beet salad. Nueske's bacon is the star in a rustic BLT, accompanied by Klug Farms peaches tossed with balsamic dressing. Finally, cream cheese-frosted carrot bread pudding is fragrant from autumn spices, layered with a golden raisin purée and nutmeg crunch.

- 228 W. Chicago Ave. (bet. Franklin & Wells Sts.)
- Chicago (Brown)
- (312) 280-4960 — **WEB:** www.farmhousechicago.com
- Lunch & dinner daily   **PRICE: $$**

THE FRANKLIN ROOM

American • *Tavern*

                                            MAP: C2

With a motto like "Ladies and Gentlemen Welcome," it's no surprise that the subterranean space housing this modern-day tavern and whiskey bar is as inviting as they come. Surrounded by backlit bottles of top-notch spirits under wrought-iron latticework light panels, guests gather for convivial conversation and great drinks.

Fans of Bourbon will delight in the Derby Day Mule, which swaps out vodka for Buffalo Trace. Brown spirits are celebrated; note that hefty supply of Pappy Van Wickle. Pair your libation with a snack of parmesan-battered cauliflower tots with blue cheese dressing before tucking in to the delightfully rich squid ink seafood pasta tossed in a pesto cream sauce. End on a high note—think Bourbon-infused milkshake with house-made ice cream.

675 N. Franklin St. (bet. Erie & Huron Sts.)
Chicago (Brown)
(312) 445-4686 — **WEB:** www.franklinroom.com
Lunch Mon – Fri Dinner nightly   **PRICE:** $$

FRONTERA GRILL

Mexican • *Colorful*

                                              MAP: D3

The linchpin in Rick Bayless' empire, Frontera Grill is decidedly unique in its homage to regional Mexican cuisine and displays a near cult-like devotion to local product. The service at this dining room, psychedelic in its color scheme, can verge on vapid, but find a seat on the bar side for a warmer (and worthier) experience.

The ever-changing menu is cohesive with a mix of classics and specialties like sopa azteca, a nourishing pasilla chile broth poured atop crisp tortilla strips, cool avocado, grilled chicken and jack cheese. A version of the classic from Morelia, enchiladas a la plaza are first flash-fried, then folded over seasoned cabbage, potatoes and carrots. Pair this plate with a side of spinach in green chile and you won't be unhappy. Ever.

445 N. Clark St. (bet. Hubbard & Illinois Sts.)
Grand (Red)
(312) 661-1434 — **WEB:** www.rickbayless.com
Lunch & dinner Tue – Sat   **PRICE:** $$

GILT BAR

Gastropub • Brasserie

MAP: C4

It's not easy to miss the revolving door entrance to Gilt Bar, a moody and imposing retreat. The bar up front mixes cocktails to a metronomic rhythm, while the back feels more intimate with studded leather banquettes and nostalgic lighting.

However make no mistake: this is no Bugsy Malone speakeasy, but a grown-up version for aficionados with astute palates. Snack on smoky Brussels sprouts finished with a Dijon vinaigrette and dusting of pecorino, before savoring ricotta gnocchi tossed in nutty brown butter sauce with butternut squash, chives and parmesan. For the finale, diner-style pies are all the rage. Gorge on a coconut-cream rendition topped with pleasantly bitter coffee-infused ice cream and chocolate sauce—perhaps to the tunes of Bob Dylan? Bliss.

- 230 W. Kinzie St. (at Franklin St.)
- Merchandise Mart
- (312) 464-9544 — **WEB:** www.giltbarchicago.com
- Dinner nightly   **PRICE: $$**

GIORDANO'S

Pizza • Family

MAP: F1

Value, friendly service, and iconic deep-dish pizza make Giordano's a crowd sweetheart among locals and tourists alike. With locations dotting the city and suburbs, this spot has been gratifying locals with comforting Chicago-style Italian-American fare for years. Come during the week—service picks up especially at dinner—to avoid the cacophony.

The menu includes your typical salads and pastas, but you'd do well to save room for the real star: the deep-dish. Bring backup because this pie could feed a small country. The spinach version arrives on a buttery pastry crust, filled with sautéed (or steamed) spinach with tomato sauce and topped with mozzarella and parmesan. For those cold, windy nights, opt for delivery—their website sketches a detailed menu.

- 730 N. Rush St. (at Superior St.)
- Chicago (Red)
- (312) 951-0747 — **WEB:** www.giordanos.com
- Lunch & dinner daily   **PRICE:** 🍴

GT FISH & OYSTER

Seafood • Chic

MAP: C3

Quaint seaside shacks have nothing on this nautical-chic urban spot. A boomerang-shaped communal table by the raw bar makes a perfect perch for slurping oysters. Lead fishing weights keep napkins in place on brass-edged tables, arranged beneath a chalkboard mural of a jaunty swordfish skeleton. Pescatarians savor the seafood dishes meant for sharing, but those who forgo fish are limited to three meat options. Start with tuna poke dressed in soy sauce, sesame oil and ginger with shaved cucumber. Then move on to deep-fried oysters topped with kimchi and served in a soft slider bun. Carrot cake with orange buttercream, pineapple purée and coconut ice cream is pure bliss.

Steak lovers should stop by GT Prime, lauded for its luxurious setting and unique cuts.

- 531 N. Wells St. (at Grand Ave.)
- Grand (Red)
- (312) 929-3501 — **WEB:** www.gtoyster.com
- Lunch Tue – Sun Dinner nightly   **PRICE:** $$

HUBBARD INN

American • Tavern

MAP: D3

Handsome from head-to-toe, Hubbard Inn takes the idea of a classic tavern and dresses it to the nines. Brass-clad globe lights glow above lacquered plank tables in the front bar room, leading to tufted leather couches and fireplaces in the book-lined and Hogwarts-worthy library. The second floor is low-slung and loungy. A wall-sized chalkboard behind the marble bar whets whistles with descriptions of cocktails.

The kitchen's shareable dishes appeal to nearly every appetite. And while ubiquitous items like lamb meatballs or grilled octopus salad lean toward the Mediterranean, Maine lobster roll or bison burger with pickled raspberries are all-American. Brunch offerings like fried chicken with buttermilk biscuits have garnered a cult-like following—natch.

- 110 W. Hubbard St. (bet. Clark & LaSalle Sts.)
- Merchandise Mart
- (312) 222-1331 — **WEB:** www.hubbardinn.com
- Lunch & dinner daily   **PRICE:** $$

THE KITCHEN

American • Chic

MAP: D4

Panoramic views and eye-popping spaces are par for the course at most of the lofty spots abutting the Chicago River, but The Kitchen's farm-to-table food manages to steer the focus back to the plate. The restaurant's approachable, community-minded take on straightforward seasonal food—along with its impressive drinks program—makes it easy to please.

Even if you're not attending a Monday "Community Night" dinner alongside many of the purveyors whose ingredients appear on the plate, you'll find a fresh, flavorful mix of dishes. Crushed white bean bruschetta is topped with a sprightly herb and frisée salad, which is in turn dressed with a blood orange vinaigrette. And wild Bristol Bay salmon is poached with care, its silkiness punctuated by garlic-chive aïoli.

▢ 316 N. Clark St. (bet. Kinzie St. & the Chicago River)

▢ Merchandise Mart

𝒫 (312) 836-1300 — **WEB:** www.thekitchenbistros.com

▢ Lunch & dinner daily **PRICE:** $$

MASTRO'S

Steakhouse • Luxury

MAP: E3

Mastro's takes its perch in the Windy City's steakhouse scene with the swagger of an old pro. Black SUVs unload VIPs in front of the revolving door, which in turn leads to a gleaming wall of bottles at the gilded bar. Live lounge music may take the level of conversation up a notch, but sip on a shaken martini to blank out the surrounding din.

Steaks on screaming-hot platters come unadorned unless otherwise listed, and servers will happily rattle off recommendations for toppings, sauces and crusts. Salads like Mastro's house version, a local favorite stocked with chopped jumbo shrimp and a giant steamed prawn, are hearty (read: oversized), but smaller portions are also on offer so you may as well leave room for their renowned butter cake.

▢ 520 N. Dearborn St. (at Grand Ave.)

▢ Grand (Red)

𝒫 (312) 521-5100 — **WEB:** www.mastrosrestaurants.com

▢ Dinner nightly **PRICE:** $$$$

PACIFIC STANDARD TIME

Californian • *Trendy*

                                               MAP: D2

Reservations are recommended at this buzzy Cal-Italian spot. Awash in bright white walls and blonde wood, including a bustling bar settled into the center of the restaurant, Pacific Standard Time brings a breezy West Coast vibe to River North, and the Midwest can't get enough.

On the menu, you'll find a refreshing mix of Neapolitan-style pizzas, homemade pastas and fish. Highlights though include the ahi tuna starter, as well as trout dressed with a Thai vinaigrette, sesame, avocado purée and dill. At the center of the kitchen are two oak wood-fueled hearths, which turn out rib-sticking items like roasted chicken and whole duck (not to mention those delicious pies).

Service is personable and casual, but highly attentive to the details that count.

■ 141 W. Erie St. (at LaSalle Dr.)
🚇 Grand
✆ (312) 736-1778 — **WEB:** www.pstchicago.com
■ Dinner nightly   **PRICE:** $$

PROSECCO

Italian • *Elegant*

                                               MAP: C2

No matter the hour, it's always time for bubbly at Prosecco, where a complimentary splash of the namesake Italian sparkler starts each meal. This fizzy wine inspires the restaurant's elegant décor, from creamy pale walls and damask drapes to travertine floors. Sit at the long wooden bar or in one of the well-appointed dining rooms for a second glass chosen from the long list of frizzante and spumante wines.

Hearty dishes spanning the many regions of Italy cut through the heady bubbles. Carpaccio selections include the classic air-dried bresaola as well as whisper-thin seared rare duck breast. Saltimbocca di vitello marries tender veal medallions with crispy Prosciutto di Parma and creamy mozzarella, with hints of sage in the tomato-brandy sauce.

■ 710 N. Wells St. (bet. Huron & Superior Sts.)
🚇 Chicago (Brown)
✆ (312) 951-9500 — **WEB:** www.prosecco.us.com
■ Lunch Mon – Fri Dinner Mon – Sat   **PRICE:** $$

RAMEN-SAN ⅃○

Asian • Minimalist

MAP: D4

Lettuce Entertain You brings you bowlfuls of ingredient-driven noodle soups served up right next door to the restaurant group's Il Porcellino. The menu at this Asian concept revolves around a handful of tastefully crafted broths dancing with Tokyo wavy noodles produced by Sun Noodle. The tonkotsu ramen, for instance, is a traditional pleasure afloat with slices of chashu, wakame and molten egg. Meanwhile, the kimchi and fried chicken ramen is a novel departure, defined by pungent fried garlic and buttered corn.

Ramen-san's loyal following is comprised of hipsters and suits alike, and they all seem to dig the salvaged look and booming playlist. Night owls take note: Japanese whiskies rule the bar and fried rice is served late into the night.

■ 59 W. Hubbard St. (bet. Clark & Dearborn Sts.)
▣ Grand (Red)
✆ (312) 377-9950 — **WEB:** www.ramensan.com
■ Lunch & dinner daily   **PRICE:** ⊖⊖

RPM STEAK ⅃○

Steakhouse • Fashionable

MAP: D4

RPM Steak shares the same sleek, moneyed vibe as still-happening RPM Italian, its sibling around the corner. Polished black, white and wood décor speaks to the finer things in life, with a menu of succulent steaks, raw bar offerings and sides to back it up. There's always a full house; for the best people-watching, score one of the semicircular booths.

While steaks range from petite filets to dry-aged 24-ounce cowboy cuts, highlights include the classic steak frites complemented by truffle béarnaise for the meat and Caesar dip for the fries. But the 90-day dry aged ribeye is easily the kitchen's most impressive, thanks to a winning seasoning salt. The serious wine list ping-pongs around the globe with nods to Napa, Burgundy and everything in between.

■ 66 W. Kinzie St. (bet. Clark & Dearborn Sts.)
▣ Merchandise Mart
✆ (312) 284-4990 — **WEB:** www.rpmsteak.com
■ Lunch Mon – Fri Dinner nightly   **PRICE:** $$$$

SIDE DOOR 🍴

Gastropub • *Tavern*

MAP: F2

In a city with no shortage of steakhouses, Side Door dares to be different. It's the casual arm of Lawry's in the historic McCormick Mansion, offering the same quality and service without the power lunch vibe. Comfy leather banquettes and wide wooden tables are well spaced throughout the bi-level restaurant, offering a respite for shoppers to relax with a cheese plate and craft beer flight.

Share an order of prime rib poutine among friends—it's drenched in beef gravy and pepper jack cheese—or go whole hog with the prime rib sandwich, which is hand-carved to order and presented tableside with horseradish cream and au jus. For something lighter but just as pleasurable, try the kale Caesar, with white anchovies and a delicately creamy garlic dressing.

 100 E. Ontario St. (at Rush St.)

Grand (Red)

☎ (312) 787-6768 — **WEB:** www.sidedoorchicago.com

Lunch & dinner daily

PRICE: $$

SIENA TAVERN 🍴

Italian • *Chic*

MAP: E4

With a glitzy bar and cozy semicircular booths, this is where rustic Italian meets contemporary glam. The service and vibe are warmer than the pizza oven open to the room. There is something for everyone on this menu, including an expansive selection of antipasti, salads and pasta. Seasonal soups are excellent, like the smooth roasted butternut squash drizzled with truffle-chestnut gremolata.

Pizzas arrive with a thin, fire-licked crust that is gently charred and puffed, perhaps creatively topped with a sauce-free mix of caramelized Brussels sprouts, roasted garlic, corn, gooey Taleggio and white truffle oil.

Brunch-time monkey bread is so sticky, sweet and oozing with caramel, candied hazelnuts and whipped cream, that it must be eaten with a spoon.

51 W. Kinzie St. (at Dearborn St.)

Merchandise Mart

☎ (312) 595-1322 — **WEB:** www.sienatavern.com

Lunch & dinner daily

PRICE: $$

SLURPING TURTLE ⅈ○
Japanese • Minimalist

♿

MAP: D3

Both turtles and noodles symbolize longevity, so a meal here should add a few years to your life (and warmth to your belly). Inside, diners sit elbow-to-elbow at sleek communal tables, but there are also a handful of booths along one wall, as well as a glass mezzanine with a view of the dining room below. Boutique beverages like Hitachino Nest beer and Ramuné bubble-gum soda bring smiles to patrons in the know.

The menu of Japanese comfort food is compact, featuring a few ramen bowls, sashimi, maki, as well as hot and cold small plates for snacking and sharing. Then bao filled with smoky-glazed pork belly and pickled veggies arrive fluffy and piping hot. It hardly gets better than the duck fat-fried chicken, a puffed up shell of fried happiness.

▨ 116 W. Hubbard St. (bet. Clark & LaSalle Sts.)
▨ Merchandise Mart
☏ (312) 464-0466 — **WEB:** www.slurpingturtle.com
▨ Lunch & dinner daily

PRICE:

STEAK 48 ⅈ○
Steakhouse • Fashionable

🎱 ♿ ⊡ 🍽

MAP: F2

Steakhouses are as prevalent as the Chicago wind in River North, but the family that founded the much-loved Mastro's shows us that they've still got some tricks up their sleeves with this popular sibling. Don't be fooled by the buzzing crowd and thumping music as Steak 48—albeit trendy—really knows how to pack them in by doling out sizzling, next-level cuts with impressive consistency.

The interior is dark, with black floors, burnt-orange booths and a sparkling glass-enclosed kitchen that showcases a massive display of seafood on ice. Well-priced and appetizing cuts of meat are the main attraction, but their notable supporting lineup of a dozen sides may include delicious double-baked truffle potatoes, generous salads and myriad fish preparations.

▨ 615 N. Wabash Ave. (bet. Ohio & Ontario Sts.)
▨ Grand (Red)
☏ (312) 266-4848 — **WEB:** www.steak48.com
▨ Dinner nightly

PRICE: $$$

SUSHI-SAN ¶○

Japanese • Minimalist

&

MAP: D3

Why cook dinner when it's all too easy to drop into this sleek retreat for a quick bite or linger with friends over sake and sips? One of the few spots in town that is open late, Sushi-San's menu is built for crowds—imagine the likes of filling rice bowls and extensive lists of maki. Charcoal-grilled proteins and vegetables, like the delicious Vietnamese Berkshire pork or charred cauliflower, also make for true-blue feasts.

The interior is hip and minimalist, furnished with wooden seats, exposed ductwork, a black ceiling and pumping hip-hop beats. A counter in the back is best for a more intimate experience with the chef. Service is friendly and efficient; and if in a rush, rest easy, as you could be in and out in under half an hour if need be.

◼ 63 W. Grand Ave. (bet. Clark & Dearborn Sts.)

▣ Grand (Red)

℘ (312) 828-0575 — **WEB:** www.sushisanrestaurant.com

◼ Lunch Mon – Fri Dinner nightly   PRICE: $$

TRAVELLE ¶○

Contemporary • Design

⊗ & ⟠ ▤ ◿ ◿

MAP: E4

This contemporary dining room shares its home—a landmark Mies van der Rohe tower completed in 1972—with The Langham Hotel. Floor-to-ceiling windows on the second-floor space offer views of Marina City, but with its stunning kitchen displayed behind gradient glass panels, the scene inside is equally dramatic.

Creative add-ins bring Mediterranean flair and flavor to flawlessly executed and gorgeously composed dishes. Seared octopus and intensely flavorful pork belly dazzle with lashes of squid ink and dots of kewpie mayo. Garlic breadcrumbs, bacon and peppercorns create a winning mix in the prettiest risotto carbonara you've ever seen. Finish with a slice of nicely crusted brown butter cake topped with cinnamon ice cream rolled in cereal flakes.

◼ 330 N. Wabash Ave. (bet. Kinzie St. & the Chicago River)

▣ Grand (Red)

℘ (312) 923-7705 — **WEB:** www.travellechicago.com

◼ Lunch & dinner daily   PRICE: $$$

TOPOLOBAMPO ✿

Mexican • Elegant

MAP: D3

This jewel in the Bayless crown welcomes a rush of serious diners for original south-of-the-border food with an upscale twist. While you have to walk through cacophonous Frontera Grill, the relative serenity that greets you is worth the detour. This bright and cheery dining room with gold curtains and colorful artwork feels worlds away from the fiesta up front.

The regional Mexican cuisine boasts a panoply of flavors, colors and textures with a finesse that is truly impressive. Lunches are laid-back and may include a quartet of quesadillas stuffed with chorizo, black beans and queso fresco. These are made even more luscious when served with a Veracruz salsa negra. "Seasonal" or "Classic" tasting menus at dinner demonstrate the kitchen's haute cuisine approach to authentic items and ingredients. Dishes are also sauced perfectly: the uni-infused spicy yellow mole poured over a single seared scallop is just one example.

Cocktails are noteworthy (margaritas, naturally), with tequila and mezcal flights, plus a concise wine list featuring Mexican labels. Teetotalers get equal attention thanks to sweet and tangy agua frescas splashed with tropical juices that are among the best in town.

▮ 445 N. Clark St. (bet. Hubbard & Illinois Sts.)

🚇 Grand (Red)

✆ (312) 661-1434 — **WEB:** www.rickbayless.com

▮ Lunch Tue – Fri Dinner Tue – Sat

PRICE: $$$$

TRUE FOOD KITCHEN
American • Contemporary décor

MAP: E2

True Food Kitchen is just what the doctor ordered—Dr. Andrew Weil, that is, who, along with "restopreneur" Sam Fox, has written a prescription for food that is as healthy as it is delicious.

Housed in a trendy part of the city and in an 8,000-square-foot loft-like space, this open and airy "kitchen" features lime-green banquettes, lemon-hued chairs and a bar that slings fresh juice cocktails like skinny citrus margaritas. The menu showcases the chef's talent for delivering next-level vegetable dishes. But carnivores may rest easy as the gluten-free chicken sausage pie, as well as the spaghetti squash casserole topped with fresh mozzarella and dressed with herbs, caramelized onions and shredded zuchinni, are bound to sate every type of palate.

■ 1 W. Erie St. (at State St.)
▧ Grand (Red)
✆ (312) 204-6981 — **WEB:** www.truefoodkitchen.com
■ Lunch & dinner daily

PRICE: $$

UNTITLED SUPPER CLUB
Contemporary • Trendy

MAP: D4

An unmarked entrance leads the way to this subterranean lair, its various rooms pumping out music and serving up hand-crafted cocktails to a cool clientele lounging in tufted leather banquettes. Lights are sultry, tables are low-slung and casual and there are no less than 507 whiskeys to choose from.

A charcuterie board may offer up silky duck rillettes, shot through with foie gras; textured and spreadable liverwurst; as well as thin slices of prosciutto and coppa accompanied by a house-made mostarda. Overstuffed squash blossom rellenos are filled with creamy ricotta and served over agave-spiked corn relish as well as chili-lime crema. Don't miss the scrumptious meatloaf sandwich, slathered with Korean-style ketchup and laced with rosemary-infused aïoli.

■ 111 W. Kinzie St. (bet. Clark & LaSalle Sts.)
▧ Merchandise Mart
✆ (312) 880-1511 — **WEB:** www.untitledchicago.com
■ Dinner Mon – Sat

PRICE: $$

WEST LOOP

GREEKTOWN · MARKET DISTRICT

Once home to scores of warehouses and smoke-spewing factories, the West Loop today is arguably the most booming part of the Windy City, whirring with sleek art galleries, attractive lofts, hopping nightclubs, and cool, cutting-edge restaurants. Young residents may have replaced the struggling immigrants of yore; nevertheless, traces of ethnic flavor can still be found along these vibrant blocks. They certainly aren't as dominant as before—what a difference a century or two can make—but

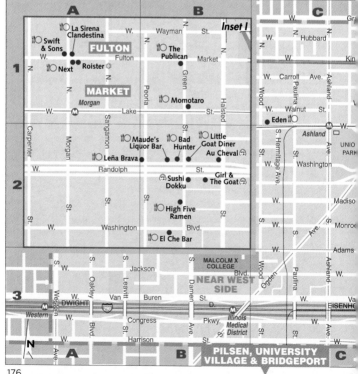

nearby Taylor Street continues to charm passersby, tourists, and residents alike with its timeless-turned-slightly kitschy feel. Imagine the likes of delis, groceries, and food stops galore and you will start to get the picture.

A MEDITERRANEAN MARVEL

For tasty, Mediterranean-inspired munching, make your way to Greektown where everybody's Greek, even if it's just for the day. Shout "opa" at the **Taste of Greektown** festival, held each August, proffering thrilling eats as well as drinks from local restaurants, and celebrating all things Mediterranean. Sound too Greek to you? Venture beyond into "Restaurant Row," situated along Randolph Street, where culinary treasures hide among beautiful, fine dining establishments. Whet

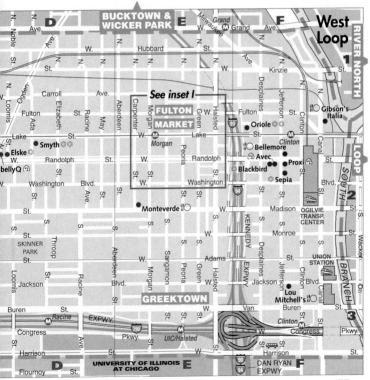

your appetite with everything from sushi to hefty subs—this mile-long sandwich breed is a best seller bursting with salty meats at **J.P. Graziano's**. Yes, the queues are long here, but rest assured that the wait is entirely worth it.

If all else fails, round-up say 1,000 of your closest friends for a meze at one of the many Moroccan spots nearby. Then chase down West Randolph's exquisite eats with intricately crafted bevvies at **The Aviary**. This bar in West Fulton Market is the brainchild of Chef Grant Achatz, and baby boy is quite the charmer indeed! Noted as much for their expert bartenders' spherical concoctions as for its tedious reservation process (this is a Kokonas business, after all!), The Aviary is also highly devoted to product quality. For even more of a scene, head downstairs to **The Office**, a super secret and super exclusive speakeasy. Then settle in for an intimate dinner at **Next's** private dining space, **The Room**.

Some carousers may choose to continue the party at **CH Distillery**, which is known to cull the finest spirits in-house.

And if that's not homegrown enough for you, this kitchen is even known to craft such delicious small plates as potato pancakes or red caviar set atop pumpernickel blinis. Nerd alert: the name CH is a double entendre indicating the molecular formula for ethanol and Chicago's very own abbreviation. Rather whip it up than wolf it down? Beef up your kitchen skills at the **Calphalon Culinary Center**, where groups can arrange for private hands-on instruction. After mastering the ever classic bœuf Bourguignon, stroll into **Peoria Packing**, a veritable meat cooler where butchers continue to slice and dice the best cuts to order. Aspiring cooks also make the rounds to Paul Kahan's **Publican Quality Meats**, another carnivorous mecca,

flooded with a mind-boggling array of specialty eats that are matched only by the spectacular setting. Think: intimate cocktail gathering-meets-extravagant dinner party. Treasure hunters will adore trolling the stalls at **Chicago French Market**, an epicurean hub and multi-use arena catering to a variety of palates. Meanwhile, health nuts won't be able to get

enough of **raw**, a grab-n-go vegan gem committed to providing the healthiest food money can buy. Moving beyond the market, even the most die-hard dieters meed a little sugar and spice, and the small plates, pastries, plus sparkling sips at the flagrantly sexy **RM Champagne Salon** is sure to fit the bill.

BEER & THE BALLGAME

Hoops fans whoop it up during Bulls games at the United Center, also home to the Blackhawks. Depending on the score, the most exciting part of the night is post-game—bingeing with buddies over beer and bar food. **The Aberdeen Tap**, for instance, is a local favorite where everybody knows your name, as well as the exceptional selection of beers on tap—they boast over 65 brews. But, be sure to also take your (more finicky) pals to **Rhine Hall**, a boutique brandy distillery run by a father-and-daughter duo. Finally, those who prefer a little brawl with their beer will fall for **Twisted Spoke**, the proverbial biker bar with tattoos and 'tudes to match. The music is loud and these drinks are plentiful, but it's all in good testosterone- and alcohol-fueled fun.

AU CHEVAL

American • *Tavern*

MAP: B2

This corner bar on Randolph Street's restaurant row may be dim, but it's got a few glittering edges. The reel-to-reel in the doorway lends a retro feel, but the rest is decidedly cushy. Late-night revelers prefer to sit at tufted leather booths or savor beers at the zinc-topped bar rather than endure a wait for a table in the raucous space. Bartenders work just as hard as line cooks until the wee hours.

The kitchen puts a highfalutin spin on simple bar eats. In-house butchers craft 32-ounce pork Porterhouses for sharing; foie gras for folding into fluffy scrambled eggs; and house-made sausages for bologna sandwiches that go well beyond a kid's wildest dreams. Thin griddled cheeseburger patties are comparably perked up by maple syrup-glazed peppered bacon.

■ 800 W. Randolph St. (at Halsted St.)
🚇 Morgan
📞 (312) 929-4580 — **WEB:** www.auchevalchicago.com
■ Lunch & dinner daily   PRICE: $$

AVEC

Mediterranean • *Contemporary décor*

MAP: F2

Fans have been clamoring for the dinner plates at this West Randolph mainstay for more than a decade—and now that lunch is on the menu, it's official: Avec is a non-stop hangout. It's a fun vibe, as diners are tightly packed at a long counter and communal seats in the chic wood plank-encased room; servers do a good job attending to the crowd.

Mediterranean flavors factor prominently in the kitchen's stimulating creations, like a kale and carrot salad dressed with delightfully herbaceous and spicy green harissa as well as sunflower seeds for crunch. A thick slice of excellent whole grain bread spread with walnut-beet muhamarra is the foundation of an open-faced roasted salmon sandwich. Other delights—there are many—come and go with the seasons.

■ 615 W. Randolph St. (bet. Desplaines & Jefferson Sts.)
🚇 Clinton (Green/Pink)
📞 (312) 377-2002 — **WEB:** www.avecrestaurant.com
■ Lunch Sun – Fri Dinner nightly   PRICE: $$

BAD HUNTER
Contemporary · Trendy

 MAP: B2

Bad Hunter is a wildly popular and exciting destination on this hip restaurant row. The sun-filled interior is light and sleek, with a soothing décor of whitewashed brick walls, caramel-hued banquettes and lush greenery to ensure that the space feels airy and never overcrowded. Servers deftly manage the room, no matter how many orders are rushing in.

The cooking unveils an inventive take on seasonal farm-to-table dining, with wood-fire roasting and fermentation playing large parts. Start with fluke crudo in tangy carrot-citronette. Then move on to saffron farfalle dressed with an ingenious root vegetable "Bolognese" so good that no one misses the meat. Desserts are another highlight, especially the caramelized white chocolate and parsnip panna cotta.

■ 802 W. Randolph St. (at Halsted St.)
■ Morgan
✆ (312) 265-1745 — **WEB:** www.badhunter.com
■ Lunch & dinner daily   PRICE: $$

BELLEMORE
Contemporary · Luxury

MAP: F2

The good folks at the Boka Restaurant Group have done it again with Bellemore, a West Loop beauty that has tongues wagging across town. Headed by the extremely talented Jimmy Papadopoulos (of Bohemian House), this menu pairs the most pristine ingredients with classical French techniques. Unsurprisingly, the results practically shine in dishes like venison tartare, paired with silky bonito aïoli, smoky trumpet mushrooms and Tokyo turnips; or a perfectly flaky oyster pie, starring caviar, crème fraîche and tart green apple.

The servers are jacketed, yet their style is friendly and personable. The buzzy interior lights up at night with convivial chatter, as guests soak in the stunning setting, lined with rounded booths and striking chandeliers.

■ 564 W. Randolph St. (at Jefferson St.)
■ Clinton (Green/Pink)
✆ (312) 667-0104 — **WEB:** www.bellemorechicago.com
■ Lunch Mon – Sat Dinner nightly   PRICE: $$$

BELLYQ

Asian · *Simple*

                                 MAP: D2

This end of West Randolph Street might be quiet, but it's always a party inside bellyQ. The volume and energy are high throughout the lofty, concrete-heavy space with tabletop-hibachi booths and industrial-metal seats. A wall-length, horse-themed screen separates the restaurant from its casual sibling, Urban Belly, which shares the open kitchen.

As imagined by prolific Chef/owner Bill Kim, the Asian barbecue experience at bellyQ takes its form in a number of genre-melding shareable plates. A side of bibimbap-style sticky rice is crunchy and tender, tossed with glistening slices of Chinese sausage and generously sprinkled with togarashi. Chewy chunks of brownie in vanilla soft-serve are drizzled with caramel-balsamic-soy "Seoul sauce" for a savory twist.

■ 1400 W. Randolph St. (at Ogden Ave.)
▣ Ashland (Green/Pink)
✆ (312) 563-1010 — **WEB:** www.bellyqchicago.com
■ Dinner nightly   **PRICE: $$**

EDEN ⑩

Contemporary · *Chic*

                                 MAP: C1

This lovely addition to the West Loop dining scene arrives thanks to husband-and-wife-team, Chef Devon Quinn and Jodi Fyfe. The gorgeous, whitewashed space offers an airy, vibrant ambience even by night, with exposed brick, encaustic tile at the convivial bar, tufted leather banquettes and commissioned artwork throughout.

The inspired cuisine applies flavors of the Mediterranean to seasonal produce, some of it plucked straight from the on-site urban garden. Renowned favorites from the menu may include baked shrimp paccheri; curried lentil brik; or even cumin-grilled lamb with Israeli couscous and merguez. House-made pastas might feature sweet pea pierogi with broccoli purée, trumpet mushrooms, pickled spring onions and crispy potato shards.

■ 1748 W. Lake St. (at Wood St.)
▣ Ashland (Green/Pink)
✆ (312) 366-2294 — **WEB:** www.edeninchicago.com
■ Lunch Sun Dinner Wed – Sat   **PRICE: $$$**

BLACKBIRD 🍀

Contemporary • Design

MAP: F2

In many ways, an acclaimed restaurant that opened in 1997 may seem like old news, but Chef/owner Paul Kahan continues to enliven this Windy City original with fresh talent and new flavor.

The interior is small but packed, right down to the last lunchtime bar stool. Everything feels glossy and white, accented with high-back leather banquettes and orange place mats that pop with color at the bar. Service is sharp, busy and handling it all very well. Begin your unique dining journey here with a warm, poached Maine shrimp "salad" tossing meaty bacon and pickled walnuts with segments of tangy orange. Then segue into a perfect marriage of salinity and sweetness by way of the ultra-crisp potato-wrapped sturgeon fillet accompanied by tender gnocchi, laid atop a bed of steamed mussels and finished with a luxurious "sauce Parisienne." Desserts at Blackbird are equally intricate and inspired, including that divine combination of crunchy apple-cider donuts with creamy cinnamon-laced ricotta, a rich mostarda, as well as a cooling scoop of buckwheat ice cream.

Dinner may be served as a ten-course tasting menu that shows just what this capable kitchen can do. Lunch is an astounding bargain.

■ 619 W. Randolph St. (bet. Desplaines & Jefferson Sts.)
🚇 Clinton (Green/Pink)
📞 (312) 715-0708 — **WEB:** www.blackbirdrestaurant.com
■ Lunch Mon – Fri Dinner nightly   **PRICE:** $$$

EL CHE BAR

Argentine • Trendy

                                                     MAP: B2

This love letter to Argentine cooking arrives courtesy of Chef John Manion (of La Sirena Clandestina), who spent much of his childhood in Sao Paulo, Brazil and traveling through South America. Look beyond the jade-green tiled exterior to find this cool hot spot. Its slender space is lined with black brick, white mortar, wood slats and leads to an enormous open-hearth oven in the rear. Tiny votives and potted plants warm the room with an of-the-moment vibe.

Wood-fired grilled fare figures largely on this menu, where you'll also uncover comfort-food favorites like golden-fried empanadas chock full of spicy beef and golden raisins. Morcilla is set over a thin purée of white beans and hit with charred shishito peppers for an added kick.

   845 W. Washington Blvd. (bet. Green & Peoria Sts.)

   Morgan

   (312) 265-1130 — **WEB:** www.elchebarchicago.com

   Dinner nightly   **PRICE:** $$$

GIBSON'S ITALIA

Steakhouse • Elegant

                                                     MAP: F1

There's a reason Gibson's Italia is a see-and-be-seen kind of place. By day, the room is flooded with sunlight and stunning panoramic views of the Chicago River. Come dinnertime, the lights dim and the twinkling cityscape offers romantic magic, while a rooftop bar with fireplace opens up in the summer. And all of that's before you even taste the delicious food.

Much like its sister restaurant in the cheeky "Viagra Triangle," this Gibson's is an old-school bastion of martinis and red meat. Classics get gussied up with contemporary Italian touches in antipasti plates like the crabmeat and avocado parfait. This menu also features aged Australian grass-fed beef and specialty cuts like the Japanese A5 sirloin from the Hy_go Prefecture, charged by the ounce.

   233 N. Canal St. (bet. Fulton & Lake Sts.)

   Clinton (Green/Pink)

   (312) 414-1100 — **WEB:** www.gibsonsitalia.com

   Lunch & dinner Mon – Sat   **PRICE:** $$$

ELSKE

Contemporary • Design

♿ ⛲ 🍴 🧼

A vivid blue neon sign marks the entry to stylish Elske, the hip and sophisticated offering brought to you by husband-and-wife chef duo, David and Anna Posey. He worked at Blackbird; she at The Publican—and what they do together in this restaurant (the name means "love" in Danish) is pure culinary magic.

The spacious setting is equal parts minimal-cool and perfectly cozy, with concrete floors, exposed brick walls and open ductwork. A lovely outdoor area offers an open-air campfire with two long benches and complimentary lap furs, designed for a pre- or post-dinner cocktail or two. Inside, communal tables abound and counter seats line a gleaming open kitchen, where the cooks serve dishes directly to customers.

The chefs' deeply creative menu offers seasonal, responsibly sourced dishes rendered with impeccable skill—the flavors carefully woven together to produce irresistible profiles. A night in the talented duo's hands might unveil tender duck liver tart in an ethereally light buckwheat crust, paired with garlicky, salted ramps. Silken ocean trout is then augmented by a vibrant vinaigrette with white asparagus, perfectly balanced crème fraîche and delicate claytonia leaves.

▨ 1350 W. Randolph Ave. (at Ada St.)
▨ Ashland (Green/Pink)
℘ (312) 733-1314 — **WEB:** www.elskerestaurant.com
▨ Dinner Wed – Sun   PRICE: $$$$

GIRL & THE GOAT

Contemporary · *Trendy*

MAP: B2

The revolving door never stops turning as Girl & The Goat's party keeps going. Even on a Monday night, guests linger for hours, shouting over the din at this sceney but always friendly stunner. Appropriately rustic wooden pillars and beams connect a warren of seating areas, from elevated platforms to banquettes to dim private corner nooks.

A pick-your-own-protein adventure, the menu is organized by ingredients with a dedicated section for goat. Start with freshly baked ham bread accompanied by smoked Swiss cheese-butter seasoned with coarse mustard and olive tapenade. End with an almost pudding-like "all leches" cake enriched with strawberry-rhubarb sorbet. The kitchen may even send out mini portions of menu items for solo diners—a truly thoughtful touch.

- 809 W. Randolph St. (bet. Green & Halsted Sts.)
- Morgan
- (312) 492-6262 — **WEB:** www.girlandthegoat.com
- Dinner nightly   **PRICE:** $$

HIGH FIVE RAMEN ⑩

Japanese · *Rustic*

MAP: B2

This re-purposed industrial setting is a hipster dining hall serving two hot foodie trends under one roof. The bulk of the sprawling space is devoted to Green Street Smoked Meats, a barbecue joint where crowds of cool kids sit side-by-side downing beers and heaps of pulled pork, brisket and Frito pie.

More worthy of attention, however, is High Five Ramen, a downstairs nook where the queue for one of its 16 seats starts early. Once inside, slurp a bowl of the signature, crazy-spicy broth. Loaded with thin alkaline noodles, a slow-cooked egg, roasted pork belly, locally grown sprouts and black garlic oil, this unique rendition is worth the burn. For sweet, icy relief, sip on a slushy tiki cocktail—then wipe your brow and dig back in.

- 112 N. Green St. (bet. Randolph St. & Washington Blvd.)
- Morgan
- (312) 754-0431 — **WEB:** www.highfiveramen.com
- Dinner nightly   **PRICE:** ⊜

LA SIRENA CLANDESTINA 🍴

Latin American • Rustic

MAP: A1

Chef John Manion may be splitting his time between El Che Bar and his first baby, La Sirena Clandestina, but he hasn't missed a beat. The décor reflects the location's warehouse roots through drafting stools at the bar, well-tread wood plank floors and rugged wood tables edged in steel. Silvery pressed-tin ceilings echo the happy din of conversation below.

Be sure to try the wonderful Brazilian bowl, filled with bomba rice, chimichurri and malagueta chili salsa (good for what ails you with its spicy kick), topped with juicy grilled hangar steak (as well as avocado, grilled chicken, or shrimp). Their empanada is a signature at lunch and dinner; there's even a breakfast version at brunch. Desserts feature a delicious buttermilk tres leches.

▮ 954 W. Fulton Market (at Morgan St.)

🚇 Morgan

📞 (312) 226-5300 — **WEB:** www.lasirenachicago.com

▮ Lunch & dinner Tue – Sun   PRICE: $$

LEÑA BRAVA 🍴

Mexican • Contemporary décor

MAP: B2

This prime Randolph Street corner is home to a one-two punch of Rick Bayless-ness—an excellent taqueria and brewery named Cruz Blanza as well as this sophisticated cantina. An open kitchen displaying open-fire cooking is Leña Brava's stimulating focal point, while a buzzing bar pouring an encyclopedic range of agave spirits, brews from next door and rare Mexican wines enhances the two-floor scene.

The kitchen's Northern Mexican-influenced menu combines the bounty of the sea with the primal joy of wood-fired cooking. Be tempted by icy seafood preparations like an aquachile of sashimi-grade diver scallops in spiced cucumber juice. Then consider hearth-roasted black cod al pastor with sweet and sour pineapple, coupled with heirloom corn tortillas.

▮ 900 W. Randolph St. (at Peoria St.)

🚇 Morgan

📞 (312) 733-1975 — **WEB:** www.rickbayless.com

▮ Dinner Tue – Sun   PRICE: $$$

LITTLE GOAT DINER

American • Family

MAP: B2

Every neighborhood needs a good diner and in the booming West Loop, this enthusiastic homage to the reliable road trip stopover fits in perfectly. The décor gives a wink and a nod to classic design with retro booths, spinning chrome barstools and blue-rimmed plates, but the top-quality materials keep it on the modern side. An all-day menu of amped-up faves can be had no matter the hour. Craving a shrimp cocktail at 7:00 A.M.? Five jumbo fried shrimp wrapped in somen noodles are ready to go. The Goat Almighty burger lives up to its name with fatty beef brisket, saucy pulled pork and a ground goat patty.

Ease the pain of waiting for a table by cooling your heels at the adjacent LG Bakery with a cup of Stumptown, s'mores cookie or Bloody Mary at the bar.

 820 W. Randolph St. (at Green St.)

🚇 Morgan

✆ (312) 888-3455 — **WEB:** www.littlegoatchicago.com

⬛ Lunch & dinner daily   PRICE: $$

LOU MITCHELL'S 🍴

American • Historic

MAP: F3

At the top of Chicago's list of beloved names is Lou Mitchell. This eponymous diner is by no means an elegant affair, but thanks to its delicious omelets and iconic crowd, it has been on the Windy City's must-eat list since 1923. Don't panic at the length of the lines: they are long but move fast, and free donut holes (one of the restaurant's signature baked goods) make the wait go faster.

Back to those omelets: they may be made with mere eggs, like everyone else's, but somehow these are lighter and fluffier, almost like a soufflé, stuffed with feta, spinach, onions or any other ingredients of your choice. They arrive in skillets with an Idaho-sized helping of potatoes. The best part? Everyone gets a swirl of soft-serve at the meal's end.

⬛ 565 W. Jackson Blvd. (bet. Clinton & Jefferson Sts.)

🚇 Clinton (Blue)

✆ (312) 939-3111 — **WEB:** www.loumitchellsrestaurant.com

⬛ Lunch daily   PRICE: ⊗

MAUDE'S LIQUOR BAR 🍴

French • Cozy

It's impossible not to love this place. The overstuffed curio cabinet and blue French metal chairs aren't true antiques, for this gorgeously disheveled and rather classy brasserie isn't as old as the mirror's arful patina would have you believe. A handsome bar mixing contemporary and classic cocktails adds to the vintage atmosphere.

Fill up on French comfort food under the glow of mismatched crystal chandeliers, or head to the second-floor bar to snack on oysters and frites. The Lyonnaise salad is downright beautiful, tossing escarole, frisée and baby romaine in chive vinaigrette beneath a soft boiled egg and chunks of grilled pork belly. Steak tartare satisfies from beginning to end, and the crème brûlée makes for a deliciously textbook finish.

- 840 W. Randolph St. (bet. Green & Peoria Sts.)
- Morgan
- (312) 243-9712 — **WEB:** www.maudesliquorbar.com
- Dinner Tue – Sat   PRICE: **$$**

MOMOTARO 🍴

Japanese • Design

MAP: B1

Boka Restaurant Group's stunning West Loop canteen embraces a fantastical view of Japanese dining. An impressive selection of imported whiskies is listed on a retro-style departure board; a private dining room upstairs is styled to resemble a mid-century corporate boardroom; and a traditional izakaya beckons diners downstairs. Consistently packed, this impeccably designed space boasts numerous kitchens churning out a range of dishes.

Creative bites abound in the omakase, including torched baby squid wrapped in nori. Then a Hawaiian seaweed salad with diced nopales may be followed by robata-grilled Wagyu skirt steak with foie gras, shisito pepper and yuzu kosho. The steamed yuzu pudding cake is just one example of the surprisingly strong dessert roster.

- 820 W. Lake St. (at Green St.)
- Morgan
- (312) 733-4818 — **WEB:** www.momotarochicago.com
- Dinner nightly   PRICE: **$$$**

MONTEVERDE

Italian • *Trendy*

MAP: E2

Chef Sarah Grueneberg is a local celebrity, so expect her offspring to be packed to the last dining counter stool by 5:30 P.M. Then again this is prime seating, because behind that wood-grain bar lies the pasta station where sheets are rolled, cut and hung to dry before appearing on your plate. Her signature Italian cooking—or cucina tipica as the menu lists it—is what draws crowds.

That said, this menu is about more than just pasta, beginning with an extraordinary yet humble vessel displaying neat little bundles of cabbage leaves stuffed with herbed breadcrumbs, mushrooms and served in an inky-dark porcini Bolognese. "Wok-fried" orecchiette are also pleasantly toothsome, slicked with spicy tomato sauce and topped with gorgeously fresh head-on shrimp.

 1020 W. Madison St. (at Carpenter St.)

🚇 Morgan

✆ (312) 888-3041 — **WEB:** www.monteverdechicago.com

Dinner Tue – Sun   **PRICE:** $$

NEXT

Contemporary • *Fashionable*

MAP: A1

Welcome to dinner as theater, where the only thing more radical than each new theme is the success (or failure) of the cuisine. Whether you come for meals that recreate ancient Rome, Hollywood or The World's 50 Best, it makes a fun night. These culinary topics are not just unique, but also very thoughtful and thereby have diners waiting to see what's cooking with each reveal.

This year began with a French classique menu sporting old-school dishes like buttery poached turbot Normandy and supreme de poussin albufera, a delight of a dish with a sliver of chicken tucked with black truffle and paprika-flecked albufera sauce. The silver cup of rich, creamy macaroni layered with pigeon and more black truffle grabbed attention with its intensely earthy flavor.

953 W. Fulton Market (at Morgan St.)

🚇 Morgan

✆ N/A — **WEB:** www.nextrestaurant.com

Dinner Wed – Sun   **PRICE:** $$$$

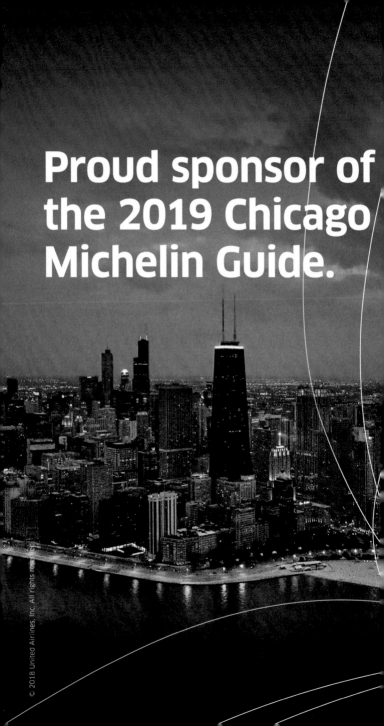

Proud sponsor of the 2019 Chicago Michelin Guide.

UNITED
AIRLINES

Cuisine and travel have always gone
hand-in-hand, and a superior experience
in either one is worth celebrating.

That's why we're excited to team up
with the *Michelin Guide North America*
as their Official Airline sponsor, serving
Chicago, New York, San Francisco
and Washington, D.C.

fly the friendly skies

PROXI 👻

International • *Contemporary décor*

MAP: F2

Here at Proxi, Chef Andrew Zimmerman seems intent on presenting his diners with a culinary whirlwind that blows from Thai beef salad to coal-roasted oysters with ssamjang butter and beyond. Otherworldly highlights reveal delicate duck dumplings floating in a pho broth with fried shallots and aromatic herbs. Regardless of the dish's inspiration, it's sure to be delicious in this kitchen's capable hands. Desserts, like avocado mousse, are made with formidable talent.

The massive room is effortlessly cool and sleek, with blue-tiled columns set beneath the white-vaulted ceiling. It also features an open kitchen and myriad seating options for everyone—from solo diners to large groups. A front lounge is ideal for lingering and waiting for your party to arrive.

- 565 W. Randolph St. (at Jefferson St.)
- Clinton (Green/Pink)
- ✆ (312) 466-1950 — **WEB:** www.proxichicago.com
- Dinner Mon – Sat

PRICE: $$

THE PUBLICAN 🍴

Gastropub • *Tavern*

MAP: B1

Everything about this West Loop favorite screams happy place—and scream you might have to, but the noisy din is all part of the fun at The Publican. Make your way inside to find a dining concept based on century-old public houses marked by lively political conversations mingled with beer in equal parts.

Each item on the menu has its place of origin listed next to it: cobia caught in Destin, FL; or lettuce grown in Buckley, MI. Global flavors make a guest appearance too, like jamón Serrano from Salamanca, Spain. Portraits of pigs hang above the wooden booths that line the room, and sure enough, pork is a highlight on the menu. Braised pork belly, for instance, is flash-fried and laid over sunchoke purée with blanched fava beans for a spectacular finish.

- 837 W. Fulton Market (at Green St.)
- Morgan
- ✆ (312) 733-9555 — **WEB:** www.thepublicanrestaurant.com
- Lunch Sat – Sun Dinner nightly

PRICE: $$$

ORIOLE ❀ ❀

Contemporary • Elegant

❀ ♿

Welcome to one of Chicago's greatest restaurants. The interior is mod yet industrial, with an open kitchen—filled with jovial professionals who look like they're cooking for a dinner party—that takes up a good deal of the space. The fact that nothing feels stuffy should not surprise since Oriole is something of a family business. Crisp attention to detail is clear from every member of this team, who are all thoroughly versed in the intricacies of the rather complex menu.

Oriole's tasting menu is stimulating and utterly contemporary; borderless with its interweaving of global flavors. It all begins with a cavalcade of delicate small bites: Maine sea urchin nigiri dabbed with spicy yuzu kosho and a Beausoleil oyster paired with a crunchy pastry cylinder wrapped in jamón Mangalica. Cumin-crusted Berkshire pork in raita is falling-off-the-bone-tender and reminiscent of India, while Hudson Valley foie gras is paired with a sea scallop for a decadent twist on surf and turf. The petite croissant filled with cheese and rosemary-apple butter will have you begging for a basket full of the diminutive delights.

Oriole thinks of everything; there is even a non-alcoholic beverage pairing on offer.

▪ 661 W. Walnut St. (at Union Ave.)

▣ Clinton (Green/Pink)

✆ (312) 877-5339 — **WEB:** www.oriolechicago.com

▪ Dinner Tue – Sat   PRICE: $$$$

SUSHI DOKKU

Japanese • Neighborhood

MAP: B2

Creatively adorned nigiri is the featured attraction at this hip sushi-ya that's all wood planks, stainless steel, chunky tables and hefty benches.

Just one piece of Sushi Dokku's supple cuts showcasing quality and technique is not enough—thankfully each nigiri order is served as pairs. Among the terrific selection, enjoy the likes of hamachi sporting a spicy mix of shredded Napa cabbage, daikon and red chili; or salmon dressed with a sweet ginger-soy sauce and fried ginger chips. South Pacific sea bream is deliciously embellished with a drizzle of smoky tomato and black sea salt. Those who wish to branch out from sushi should go for takoyaki (crispy fried octopus croquettes), grilled hamachi collar or a brownie-crusted green tea-cheesecake.

■ 823 W. Randolph St. (at Green St.)

🚇 Morgan

☎ (312) 455-8238 — **WEB:** www.sushidokku.com

■ Lunch Tue & Fri Dinner Tue – Sat   **PRICE: $$**

SWIFT & SONS ⅰ○

Steakhouse • Elegant

MAP: A1

With the inception of this large steakhouse at 1K Fulton, NY-based design firm AvroKO adds to their local portfolio in collaboration with the Boka Restaurant Group. A renovated meat and produce warehouse built in the 1920s, this space unwinds from a raw bar aptly named Cold Storage into a plush hangout. Here, wood-trimmed arches and concrete columns modulate the scale of the rooms. The kitchen's contemporary take on steak serves up USDA Prime beef seared at high heat and presented with a trio of sauces. It's the kind of place where gluttony is rewarded—even the wine list features Coravin selections in three- or six-ounce pours. Extras like King crab Oscar or dessert (Boston cream pie?) are worth the calories.

Lunch is offered on weekdays at Cold Storage.

■ 1000 W. Fulton Market (at Morgan St.)

🚇 Morgan

☎ (312) 733-9420 — **WEB:** www.swiftandsonschicago.com

■ Dinner nightly   **PRICE: $$$$**

ROISTER
Contemporary • Rustic

MAP: A1

Unapologetically loud, laid-back, and lively, Roister is part of chef Grant Achatz's culinary campus, with Next and Aviary enjoying next-door status in these former warehouse spaces. Even the ambient design reminds one of its sibling restaurants, though the cooking here, courtesy of Chef Andrew Brochu, is far more rustic.

The kitchen is boldly incorporated into the dining room and serves as its main focal point, adding to the synergy between front and back of house. Even service is a collaboration here. The best seats are along the counter, before the kitchen's blazing hearth that gives off a sexy glow. As expected, the food is creative and modern, but it is also soulful in incorporating the wood fire. Start with snacks like smoked oysters before moving on to restorative favorites like hot and sour soup abundantly stocked with Napa cabbage and shiitake mushrooms, or the umissable hearth-baked lasagna. Share the duck with dirty rice and sausage.

If you come at brunch, the chicken and waffles is hard to pass up. Slathered in honey butter and drizzled with whiskey syrup, the hot waffle is topped with a piece of crunchy boneless fried chicken for a salty yin to its sweet yang.

■ 951 W. Fulton Market (bet. Morgan & Sangamon Sts.)

▣ Morgan

☞ N/A — **WEB:** www.roisterrestaurant.com

■ Lunch & dinner daily

PRICE: $$$

SEPIA ❀
American • Vintage

MAP: F2

Housed within a historical 19th-century print shop, this urbane, stylish but unfussy dining room does a fine job mixing original details with modern touches. Muted tones in the exposed brick walls and custom tile floors complement newer elements like floor-to-ceiling wine storage and dramatic smoke-shaded chandeliers that drip with crystals.

Though the décor may tip its hat to yesteryear, the ambience is decidedly inviting and Chef Andrew Zimmerman's cuisine is firmly grounded in the 21st century.

Settle into one of their spacious tables and look forward to a meal that reflects the delicious amalgam of American cuisine, with hints of Southeast Asian, Korean and Mediterranean tastes. But, it is at dinner when this kitchen truly shines. Gnocchi for instance may seem commonplace, but this version is memorable thanks to the flawless components and rich flavors of lamb sugo and ciabatta breadcrumbs. Chicken is downright exciting, served crisp-skinned with a buttery Albufera sauce, crumbly chestnuts, caramelized fennel and sausage. Simple-sounding desserts keep the bar high until the very end of the feast, and may include a toffee-coconut cake with chocolate ganache and burnt caramel.

▨ 123 N. Jefferson St. (bet. Randolph St. & Washington Blvd.)

▨ Clinton (Green/Pink)

✆ (312) 441-1920 — **WEB:** www.sepiachicago.com

▨ Lunch Mon – Fri Dinner nightly   **PRICE: $$$**

SMYTH ✿✿

Contemporary • *Elegant*

Housed in what looks like an unremarkable industrial building, find a setting worthy of interior design magazine covers. Once inside, head up the few stairs to arrive at Smyth; then proceed into a space, which feels so comfortable that it's easy to forget you're in a restaurant. The service staff is hospitable, down to earth and manages to keep the ambience relaxed despite Chefs John Shields and Karen Urie Shields' intense craftsmanship. Beyond, the open kitchen mixes white tiles and cutting-edge equipment with a roaring hearth fire. There is a "come as you are" feeling among the crowd here, but everyone has dressed up a bit, as if in deference to the superb meal that awaits them. Original, and at times even pleasantly experimental, this kitchen's cooking has a clear vision that is sure to meet every expectation of its versatile diners. Some dishes deliver surprises through strong and gutsy flavor combinations, like a well-aged ribeye rubbed with yeasty Marmite. Other menu items strive for subtlety, such as the dried pear "jerky."

Creativity reaches its height in the "milk chocolate" dessert, which is more of a brilliant umami-bomb than confection, served with huckleberries and shiitakes.

◾ 177 N. Ada St. (bet. Lake & Randolph Sts.)

🚇 Ashland (Green/Pink)

✆ (773) 913-3773 — **WEB:** www.smythandtheloyalist.com

◾ Dinner Tue – Sat   PRICE: $$$$

INDEXES

ALPHABETICAL LIST OF RESTAURANTS

C

D

E

F

RESTAURANTS BY CUISINE

AMERICAN

FUSION

GASTROPUB

GERMAN

INDIAN

INDONESIAN

INTERNATIONAL

ITALIAN

JAPANESE

KOREAN

LATIN AMERICAN

MACANESE

Fat Rice ⊕   85

MEDITERRANEAN

Avec ⊕   182
Ēma ⦿   163
Purple Pig (The) ⊕   136

MEXICAN

Adobo Grill ⦿   118
Big Star ⦿   39
Chilam Balam ⊕   105
DeCOLORES ⊕   144
Dos Urban Cantina ⊕   84
Frontera Grill ⊕   164
Ixcateco Grill ⦿   86
Leña Brava ⦿   189
Lonesome Rose ⊕   87
L' Patron ⦿   88
Mi Tocaya ⊕   89
Quiote ⊕   92
Sol de Mexico ⊕   94
Topolobampo ❀   173

MOROCCAN

Shokran Moroccan Grill ⦿   93

PERSIAN

Noon-O-Kabab ⦿   90

PERUVIAN

Taste of Peru ⦿   30

PIZZA

Coalfire Pizza ⦿   41
Gino's East ⦿   134
Giordano's ⦿   165
Pequod's Pizza ⦿   121
Pizzeria Bebu ⊕   76

POLISH

Staropolska ⦿   95

SEAFOOD

Angry Crab (The) ⊕ — 18
GT Fish & Oyster ⊕ — 166

SOUTHERN

Big Jones ⊕ — 18
Luella's Southern Kitchen ⊕ — 26
Pearl's Southern Comfort ⊕ — 27

SPANISH

mfk. ⊕ — 121

STEAKHOUSE

Bavette's Bar & Boeuf ⊕ — 160
Benny's Chop House ⊕ — 161
Chicago Cut ⊕ — 162
Gibson's Italia ⊕ — 186
Maple & Ash ⊕ — 73
Mastro's ⊕ — 167
Michael Jordan's ⊕ — 135
Prime & Provisions ⊕ — 136
RPM Steak ⊕ — 169
Steak 48 ⊕ — 171
Swift & Sons ⊕ — 195

THAI

Herb ⊕ — 24
Jin Thai ⊕ — 25
Sticky Rice ⊕ — 109

VEGETARIAN

Mana Food Bar ⊕ — 45

VIETNAMESE

HaiSous ⊕ — 145
Pho 777 ⊕ — 28
Pho Xe Tang - Tank Noodle ⊕ — 28

CUISINES BY NEIGHBORHOOD

ANDERSONVILLE, EDGEWATER & UPTOWN ────────────

American
gather ⬩	22
Warbler (The) ⬩	31

Belgian
Vincent ⬩	31

Contemporary
Elizabeth ✿	21
Goosefoot ✿	23

Ethiopian
Demera ⬩	20
Ras Dashen ⬩	29

French
Bistro Campagne ⬩	20

Gastropub
Band of Bohemia ✿	19
Hopleaf ⬩	24

Indian
Mango Pickle ⬩	26
Sabri Nihari ⬩	29

Korean
Gogi ⬩	22
Jin Ju ⬩	25
Passerotto ⬩	27
San Soo Gab San ⬩	30

Peruvian
Taste of Peru ⬩	30

Seafood
Angry Crab (The) ⬩	18

Southern
Big Jones ○ ... 18
Luella's Southern Kitchen ○ ... 26
Pearl's Southern Comfort ○ ... 27

Thai
Herb ⊕ ... 24
Jin Thai ⊕ ... 25

Vietnamese
Pho 777 ○ ... 28
Pho Xe Tang - Tank Noodle ○ ... 28

BUCKTOWN & WICKER PARK

American
Bristol (The) ⊕ ... 40
Cafe Robey ○ ... 40
Clever Rabbit ○ ... 41
Dove's Luncheonette ⊕ ... 43
Mable's Table ○ ... 45
Mindy's Hot Chocolate ○ ... 46
TWO ⊕ ... 51

Basque
Bar Biscay ○ ... 39

Contemporary
Presidio ○ ... 48
Schwa ✿ ... 49
Temporis ✿ ... 50

French
Le Bouchon ○ ... 44

Fusion
Mott St. ⊕ ... 46

Gastropub
Bangers & Lace ○ ... 38
Dawson (The) ○ ... 42
Owen & Engine ○ ... 47

Indian
Cumin ⊕ ... 42

Italian
Piccolo Sogno ○ ... 47
tocco ○ ... 48

STARRED RESTAURANTS ✾

BIB GOURMAND 😊

S

T

U

W

UNDER $25

Tell us what you think about
our products.

Give us your opinion

satisfaction.michelin.com

CREDITS

MICHELIN TRAVEL PARTNER

Société par actions simplifiées au capital de 15 044 940 EUR
27 Cours de l'Ile Seguin - 92100 Boulogne Billancourt (France)
R.C.S. Nanterre 433 677 721

© 2018 Michelin Travel Partner - All rights reserved
Dépôt légal august 2018
Printed in Canada - august 2018
Printed on paper from sustainably managed forests

Impression et Finition : Transcontinental (Canada)